Fransesca

A Remarkable Life

By

Katrina Pavlovsky

ISBN 978-1-77136-874-2 (print)
ISBN 978-1-77136-896-4 (ebook)

Editor Zoe Mathers
Cover design Heloise Nicholl
Typeset at SpicaBookDesign

Printed and bound in Canada by Island Blue Book Printing, Victoria B.C.
(www.islandblue.com)

Dedicated to the Loving Memory
of Fransesca

"Are ye willing to walk the way with Me?"

Preface

This is the chronological story of a remarkable person. A spiritual teacher who lived with passion and purpose. Fransesca touched the lives of many people. After seeing her, one always came away feeling uplifted.

This book offers a partial glimpse into her life that was shared with me over the course of three and a half years. Fransesca told me about her life in Detroit, Michigan, Eugene, Oregon, in San Jose, California and lastly in Toronto, Canada which was where we met in 1977.

Immediately, I was impressed by her warm and loving nature. There was a glow to her and she appeared radiant. Although there was a difference of almost fifty years in age between us, our rapport felt natural.

Fransesca was devoted to the spiritual path for fifty-four years. She was extremely dedicated and disciplined. She lived a life of service by being a metaphysical consultant, a minister, a teacher, a writer and an artist. She remained humble throughout her lifetime. It was a privilege to know her.

Her life was and continues to be a living testament to communion with the inner self. Fransesca strove to be a Christ person and was spiritually enlightened. Her teachings are timeless and consist of the deeper aspects of the spiritual path.

It is my aspiration that Fransesca's story provides the reader with a feeling of love during their time with it. The greatest gift of my life was being adopted by Fransesca as her spiritual daughter. As her adopted spiritual daughter, I was given letters, transcribed communions, meditations and excerpts of correspondence throughout the course of our relationship and I wanted to share her wisdom in them with others.

The teachings are more relevant because life became more materialistic in the 1970's and in subsequent years. With the increase in materialism spiritual discipline and study became less valued. The teachings serve as guideposts to the sincere seeker who is interested in the spiritual path.

My life was greatly enriched in many ways by meeting and knowing Fransesca. She taught me discipline, meditation and loved me unconditionally. It was a special privilege to be a student and an adopted spiritual daughter because she was the most loving person I have met. She exuded kindness and warmth. Her attunement with the Cosmic was extraordinary and continued up until the last few months of her life.

She was a Master teacher (a person who has evolved with a knowledge of universal laws and one who has achieved self Mastery) and an important Wayshower (a person representing divine qualities who shows the way). Fransesca touched the lives of numerous people wherever she lived. She was an example of a life lived with love.

She kept her word in service to her Masters. She lived humbly and in this was her greatness. She made the most difficult discipline seem simple and easy. Fransesca gave one hundred percent of herself in loving service, always finding time to bring someone comfort, joy and love. Her teachings reflect a deep inner love and the desire that others have the same soul experiences.

Her skills in communication were highly developed as the rapport with others attests. She saw the potential in others and nurtured it, connecting to their soul essence.

Fransesca was a personification of Divine love in action. Her teachings remain timeless, and alongside them, Fransesca also wrote stories: a selection of them have been included in this book. They are unedited and written in Fransesca's own words as well as being dictated by the Masters.

It is my hope that this book in some way brings inspiration for those interested in the spiritual path.

Introduction

Fransesca was born on January 26, 1904 as Erna Meyer in Michigan, Detroit. She had a younger brother, Ed, an older sister, Lu and her parents were from Germany. Almost everyone on their block was from the Old Country. In a German household everything revolved around Poppa's comfort first. Then the children and Momma's care were given attention. Their family was close and loving.

Her Momma and Poppa instilled values at an early age. Her Momma taught how to say "please" and "thank you," not to interrupt while parents are talking, to always show appreciation for things people do and to be willing to do things for others without being paid. Fransesca's Momma said people came to earth as a present from God to bring happiness to others. Then God called them home, so He could teach them about love again.

Her Poppa tempered his seeming severity with justice, honesty and forthrightness. He adored her Momma. The values that he taught his children were to never borrow money unless one had the means to pay it back, to not buy on credit and to wait until one has accumulated money for what is needed, and lastly, to repay debts. He believed that one should pay the doctor first, taxes second and after all of that, to pay for debts and household expenses.

"A man is as good as his word. If his word is no good, he is no man at all," said her Poppa.

Her Poppa opened a philatelic shop. He was known all over the world as a philanthropist. He called his store the Log Cabin Stamp Company. Her Poppa loved to talk and often out talked her Momma. Moma had a signal for "my turn" to get a chance to speak, though.

It was her brother who gave Fransesca her first diary. It held everything. Fransesca wrote in diaries as a young girl and as a young woman and called them her "dear friend." She dreamed that one day, her future daughter could read them.. She played with dolls when she was small and wanted one to be her little girl.

When Fransesca lived in San Jose, she wrote a story about Christmas in her own perspective in 1910 when she was six and a half years old. It depicts her loving home as well as the Christmas traditions practiced by her family. "Christ Mass – All Glory Be Thine!" can be found in the Appendix.

Table of Contents

Chapter One

Detroit

In 1911 when Fransesca was seven, she had three layers of petticoats and high button shoes. There was a garden playhouse for her to play in that had a table, chair, a rocker and curtained windows. Her Momma taught her manners and always said: "People know who you are by the way you act."

Her Momma met with other German ladies. Her parents were raised German Lutheran in Germany and went to church five times a week. They thought their children would decide on a religious education themselves.

Her Poppa travelled as an iron ornamental moulder. For him, the most important things were "To do unto others as you would be done by," to be honourable and trustworthy, to be kind and to be a man of your word. He also said that he didn't need any religious person to tell him how to live or what to do.

For this reason, Fransesca didn't have any religious training. In 1913, at age nine, she baptized herself because she didn't want to be a sinner. She wondered who Jesus was, what He looked like and whether He would like her.

In 1914 or 1915 when Fransesca was eleven or twelve she was skinny and was always scared of being a wallflower at a party. She would refuse to go and just sat in the corner while everyone else had a boyfriend or was dancing. She wondered whether any of the boys would ask her to dance. Her Momma encouraged her to go and said, "Find another little girl who is just as scared as you are and talk to her. Be her friend. Find a friend." Fransesca went and met another skinny girl, they danced and then two boys asked them to dance. They had fun. She remained friends with this girl until she was sixteen years old. Fransesca never forgot her Momma's lesson.

In 1919 at age fifteen, Fransesca was more detailed in the writing of her diaries, stating that when she married and had a little girl, she would have all this so she would know how her Momma talked. Every boyfriend's name, everything they went to as a family and all gifts were listed in the diaries as well as her emotions.

> I gave up my diary writing because the world was "adopted" as my children, sisters, families, etc. Then the spiritual life – church, doing for others filled a vital spot but always was the child need of that special dream daughter. Irene filled it. (1946). The Cosmic finally got through to me that the WORLD was to be my mothering place – that the wee souls with their problems, growths, needs were to become my place to serve them and love them. All of a sudden I had children everywhere.
>
> Then came the big joy of realizing something very powerfully, what tremendous effect my mama's and papa's words, training, etc. had affected me and I prayed if only I could be like my mama, not so serious like papa. And lo, I am a

combination of both of them and so I have 'mama'd' lots of children in many places.

In 1928 the Philatelic and Numismatist Association had a convention in Michigan with delegates from all over the world. Fransesca and her Poppa were members. A gala was held at the Book Cadillac Hotel.

Her Momma couldn't read or write English and gave a speech for the first time. The topic was about keeping one's word and promises and how it was very important. The Philatelists were called "stampers." Her Momma gave a humorous portrayal of the philatelists. Her Poppa was afraid beforehand but her Momma did a wonderful job with the speech. The message was that:

"Mortals are always faced with situations which are easy to accept – in the moment yet when the time of facing them arrives, it is simpler to side step them. The routine path is easy, comfortable and familiar, so through habit man retreats into the easy path. God can, He does, He is and He never says I can't."

God says 'Let us try new horizons, spread our wings, survey what we have created. We must become! We must replenish the earth – we will plant our seeds and each one shall be named after me – I can!'

This excerpt was written years later upon reflection of her Momma. Fransesca wrote a poem at this time:

God is speech, God is thought
(there is naught where God is naught)
He is life. He is love
(He is within and up above)
God is vibration and every action
(He is filled with satisfaction)

God is freedom without strings
(And he soars on angel wings)
God is liberty unrestrained by man
(He's the one who says 'I can.')

In 1918 and 1919 at age fourteen and fifteen, Fransesca applied for jobs in the automotive industry and began working. However, she used her lunch hour to look for other employment.

On June 10, 1922 at age eighteen, Fransesca married Paul. She had two jobs because she and her husband didn't have much money. Fransesca learned to sew and make her own clothes and also how important it was not to hurt another person's feelings. She felt it was best to give a compliment rather than to criticize another.

She wanted to be a mama and unfortunately was not able to carry her babies to full term. After seven years of trying, she gave birth to a son on December 30, 1928 who weighed about eleven pounds. Her Momma helped to deliver him. When she held her baby, she thought no one had ever had such a beautiful child.

Her Momma massaged the baby's head to shape it. Nothing in her entire life could compare to the feeling of when he was laid in her arms. Fransesca had so many beautiful and very sad memories. There was love in all of them. She felt there was some very special dispensation and some agreement by the Heavenly ones that one special and certain one would be created. She asked how she could repay this.

"There is only one begotten for everyone. Our relationship to our God is then dependent upon our adoption to Him, to what is being taught. When we feel begotten, 'That's because love is there. God so loved the world that He gave the only begotten son to the world."

In 1931, when Fransesca was twenty-seven, she and her husband and son lived in a six-room house. Her husband didn't have a job while she worked a night shift job from eight p.m. to two a.m. She would then come home at three a.m. She would go to bed at four a.m. and sleep until eight-thirty a.m. At twelve noon Fransesca would take her son to her Momma's and then go to her other job from one-thirty p.m. to four thirty p.m. Fransesca did this for one and a half years. Regulating time made it possible to maintain this routine.

Fransesca had an icebox, not a fridge. One day, she baked a lemon pie and put it in the icebox. When she went to serve it, there were shoes on top of it! Her son, Roland said that "at daddy's work men nailed shoes down." He wanted to hide the shoes from his daddy.

In 1933, her son developed leukemia. Fransesca had a Toledo apartment with Roland so that he could receive injections. The doctors thought they had a miracle cure. Roland's health deteriorated and he died at age five. Fransesca prayed when Roland died. She didn't have any money for a funeral and called her Momma and Poppa. The funeral director came anyway. When Roland passed on, Fransesca saw the silver cord leave his body.

Fransesca visited her Momma regularly. Her Mama would ask her "To tell something funny." Fransesca would then forget what it was she wanted to tell her for the laughter cured it.

> All my younger years in Detroit were my fishing expeditions. At the drop of a hat if someone said, 'let's go fishing' I was right with it. It didn't matter if I caught a fish (though I was pretty good at it). The important part was being in the rowboat with the water all about me, just

> drifting. It was one place in the whole world (at that time) that I could LOSE the world and just be united with water, sky and ME!

In 1938, when Fransesca was thirty-four years old when her Momma passed away. Her Poppa had no goal to live. She was his sun, moon, and stars. His everything. They were romantically in love for all of their married years. He had the stamp shop but then one day his lung collapsed. His Philatelic shop downtown became his love. His all. Fransesca worked with her Poppa and could hardly pry him away from his store. It was all he had: the many customers, someone to talk to, something in which he could be active. When his health deteriorated he said, "it's no use to live – they have now taken my store." Two days later he closed his eyes.

In 1928 Fransesca started to see lights and this started her spiritual search. She was determined to find the truth and to see only Light. For four months she saw forms and experienced involuntary clairvoyance. She lived in two worlds at the same time. For three days she saw a man robed in white wearing a white turban. Magnetic blue eyes observed her during the meal. Fransesca would see a light around things. She had no awareness of the invisible world.

In 1937 Fransesca had the only mortal teacher she ever had for three and a half months: "She lived what she was – she was spiritual, from the top of her hair to her toes. She was nothing else but wonderful." She told Fransesca, "You are going to live near the mountains – you will teach – you will become a minister – you will have a church."

When Fransesca shared about her son's death and her husband being out of work, her teacher replied, "Honey, don't worry about what he says or others say, just remember how you act and what 'you' say." Fransesca also wondered why it was up to her and not others. Her teacher said, "Honey – remember always that YOU are building character. Let them worry about theirs, just remember yours!"

Fransesca spent thirty-six years searching. She experienced trials of persecution, denial, sacrifice, adoration, frustration, despair and joy.

"The Pearl is the union with the personal Master and the love from the Divine plane. It is all worth it!" She became his channel. Great dedication and compliance were needed to have soul-to-soul communion: "Service and devoted attention through obedience with love and Master manifestation as the motive are the requisites for Master channeling."

Her "mortal mission" was to instill higher goals and precepts in others, in hope that they might become channels for words of Light and in ways of love. The relationship is one of the invisible with the visible.

Fransesca met Sri Dass who taught yoga, meditation and concentration. He was the author of a book, "*Your Hidden Treasures*" published in 1944. Sri Dass wrote about happiness, vibration and self-realization.

Sri Dass gave instructions for changing unwanted habits. A person was to take an unhappy thought for an hour and then avoid thinking about it for one week. He also spoke of sealing one's consciousness to all negativity. He taught others about creating a picture of beauty. For example, imagining nature. The subconscious mind is impressed by what one sees and thinks about.

Sri Dass taught a chant to use when conditions or people are upsetting. This consists of walking around the parameters of a room singing Aum to the melody of "do re mi" in the following sequence: "do re mi, do re mi, do re, do." When completed, one is to walk backwards out of the room in the house or apartment. Doing so clears the energy.

Some years later Fransesca raised forty German Shepherds. She began her day at five a.m. to prepare the food. She used to buy fifty pounds of spare ribs on a weekly basis and would cook them down and grind them into bone meal. Vegetables were cut up and forty loaves of bread were baked into crusty chunks.

Fransesca would take the lead dog and twenty others on a leash four times a day to teach them how to act in public. Those interested in buying a German Sheppard would sometimes stay for two to three hours. Fransesca checked on the new owners on a monthly basis for up to one year because she wanted to see that her pups were being well handled and fed.

From three p.m. to four p.m. in the afternoon, for one hour a day, was Fransesca's time to do as she wished. She maintained this practice for many years. Fransesca became dedicated to the Cosmic (the Divine intelligence that is in everything) as of 1928.

She met Harry at work. They dated and when Fransesca was ready, she gave her consent for marriage. She and Harry Moore married and they moved to Oregon.

Chapter Two

Oregon

From 1945 to 1958 Fransesca lived on Green Hill, Oregon in the United States. In 1947, she and her husband built their own home. It was situated seven miles from Eugene. They even built Harry's shop next to their home which was for clock and watch repairs. The property consisted of a large, eighty-foot rock garden. The home overlooked Eugene, a lake and a valley beyond and below. In the distance, there was a coastal mountain range. The hilltop stood at one thousand feet above elevation.

Three sides of the house had floor length windows. There was a large kitchen with an adjoining fruit room. Fransesca's husband loved her cooking and often invited guests for dinner on short notice. She and her husband installed electric heat in the house. Fransesca also had collections of coloured glass and vases.

The house had a forested area that was five hundred feet between Fransesca's home and her neighbour's. There was also a half-acre of flowers, which required five to six hours of weeding daily. Deer and fawns visited the rose garden but never touched a leaf. Quails came to the rock garden and one year sixteen quails visited with their young.

Sunset was at four in the afternoon and the sun took four and a half hours to set. The sunsets ranged from a deep violet to a rose, apricot and salmon. At sunset Fransesca prayed and directed healing. She practiced a form of what is known as absent healing to those who had various conditions.

She also magnetized water. Fransesca felt that her home was in a sacred spot and had a feeling that she lived on this hilltop in another lifetime.

Harry did watch and clock repairs but was also a watchmaker. People came to see him in the middle of the night during the war. Fransesca began staying up all night and went to bed at 6 a.m. She kept this habit up for the rest of her life.

Fransesca became a minister and had a church. She worked in her Sanctum every day for anywhere from five to ten times even if only for fifteen minutes at a time. She prepared for it ahead of time. "I cooked all my meals as early as possible in the morning so that I could have more time in the Sanctum." She managed her time well in order to accomplish this.

Fransesca also did deliveries for her husband five times a week. During her years on Green Hill, Fransesca made seven applications for adoption, but was not successful.

Fransesca had pet cockatiels who rode on her shoulder ninety percent of the time. Pets continued to play a vital role in her life. Fransesca was a detailist and kept records. For thirty-two years she kept figures of heating costs. An article about this was published in the local paper.

Her brother Ed visited Fransesca once for fifteen days. He was hoping to retire in another nine months but three months later at age fifty-six, he had a severe heart attack. Three days later he passed on.

In 1946 Fransesca started receiving information from "Amhadra," (a Master). In an ancient language his name means "beloved son who pleases me."

In Oregon, strict discipline became a part of Fransesca's daily life. "As time went along and deeper teaching took place – the realities began to unfold and the deeper truths revealed more and more." Years of training and preparation followed. Fransesca was guided to clear out the subconscious mind. She would go into the Sanctum to verbally confess her misdeeds, thoughts and actions.

She was taught to go over her entire day to see how she had been at bedtime. What was said, how it was said, what was annoying, how did Fransesca react and if any amends could be made. It was a tough series of testing, but because Fransesca loved the Masters more than anything else in the whole world, she went through the routine. For those months, she gave thanks daily:

> ...for the Christ spirit becomes the Christ mind thereby becoming the Christ consciousness, and spirit, being part of all things – has varying forms of consciousness and the forms move and walk upon the earth in their varying stages of becoming...the spirit moves through that one, until it becomes as a fully blown Christ consciousness. When it becomes conscious of being a Christ consciousness, then is the very being of that Soul Ego – a Christ for it has attended to Home – when it was conscious of being.
>
> The conversations together each night were vitally important, for they become the nourishment to the life of Erna

> and the food for her soul. This is the nourishment of the Christ within the body.

The spiritual conversations were Fransesca's nourishment.

> ...the Christ of oneself – the Christ of everyone's self is so close to the God self, to that very Lights of the Light of the Christ...this must predominate until it is the ENTIRE DOMINANCE of one's ENTIRE Self. Not just spasmodically...but so that it becomes the complete radiation of One's soul personality – then we know that this is the Son of God which is born. This is the Inner Birth – but it becomes a mental inner realization, for Christ – the Spirit and the mind of one's self must FILL the mind – the consciousness, and this consciousness perceives the Father.

Fransesca recorded her meditations on a tape recorder and then transcribed them on a typewriter. She had questions that she would ask in her meditations and discussions. The meditations were very in depth, holy and sacred. Fransesca kept trying and was rewarded by love. She walked with God every day and experienced perfect union. Fransesca was taught many spiritual lessons and soul sensing was often involved:

> When the flesh and the psychic are one, then there is a subjugation of the five senses, as ALL senses are but one sense or 'soul sensing.' There is no outer or inner man, all one whole man. When this has come about the mortal recognizes that they see, hear, feel, sense, taste only through the one sense organ – which we speak of as Soul Sensing."

Fransesca was taught about the Christ Light and its vibration. She also learned that the Christ of one's self is the Christ of everyone's self. Her love for Jesus ran deep, and she cried tears of joy and gratitude in her meditations.

During her training years in Oregon, Fransesca spent nine months at a time on a different area such as drawing, singing and playing the piano.

Spiritual discipline was of primary importance to her. She taught with love and desire for others to "have same soul experiences and same realizations." She was a true channel for the Cosmic, a true channel of love. However Fransesca had no one to talk to about her experiences in person.

Fransesca had a very close friend, Irene whom she adopted as her spiritual daughter. They wrote letters to one another. Irene helped Fransesca to have more confidence in herself. In 1961, Irene moved to Alaska because of her husband. Eventually, Irene became sick, which in time led to a diagnosis of cancer.

In an excerpt from a letter that Fransesca wrote Irene on November 19, 1958 obeying natural law is mentioned:

> There comes a time when we haven't obeyed those laws in the beginning, where we find ourselves in such a condition that we must resort to physical means of assisting a physical condition...so it is with humans who have let the body organisms get out of control – and not followed all the laws of right living in every manner – they are in fact out of harmony with the psyche and the body – and then mind, though all powerful is expected to take care of the conditions which the Being has brought upon themselves.

Fransesca's husband became ill and in order to find release Fransesca would go to a tree and let go of the thoughts within, "It is important to let it out." It is important to get it outside of ourselves. Harry was later transferred to a sanatorium and on

November 4, 1957 he passed. Fransesca hardly had any money and had to sell canned fruits and her collection of glassware. After eight months she received a widow's veteran cheque for $50.40 a month. Harry's funeral was paid for by the Masons as Fransesca had no means to do so.

Following Harry's passing, for five weeks Fransesca couldn't be bothered to do very much. Gradually, her friends began to call, she taught a class, an electrician did the wiring and lighting for no charge, and someone came to the house to buy all of Harry's suits.

Irene's son George lived in Harry's shop after Harry died. For eight months he and Fransesca sat almost every night to exchange what they could feel, learn and see. Their rapport was one hundred percent.

Fransesca's Master advised that she move to San Jose. It took one year to sell her home on Green Hill but it was difficult for her to leave. She loved the hilltop and the surrounding area. She spent many happy years there.

Chapter Three

San Jose

Fransesca travelled to San Jose in her car and arrived there on June 23, 1959. She lived there from 1959 to 1964. Initially, she rented a furnished apartment. On her second day there she broke both knee caps. Her landlords helped her.

She was guided to hand out leaflets about starting metaphysical classes. The classes consisted of teachings, lessons and meditations. The first class was held on September 29, 1959 which was attended by fourteen people.

It was in San Jose that she took the name Fransesca. It was a suggestion by her Master (an invisible Master whose being is perceived in the Cosmic) that she do so. This name gave her strength and assurance. For six months Fransesca studied names and the value of consonants and vowels.

Fransesca said, "it takes courage to believe that thy will be done." She had to use her savings account during the beginning of her relocation. She later started giving consultations, transcribed meditations and Akashic readings for people.

She felt that it was important to give fully in service and was asked by her Master, "Are ye willing to walk the way with ME?" She also remembered that Master Jesus said, "Forsake ye all even your father and your mother and follow ME and be fishers of men!"

Fransesca often felt lonely and practiced touching her heart asking that Master Jesus be with her: "He always answers and is there in the pillow of your heart." The classes eventually became "closed classes." Eighteen devoted, dedicated and sincere students attended regularly. For three years, Fransesca conducted the classes that dealt with deeper subjects. Namely, on consciousness, workings and functioning of our bodies and the descent into matter of the soul personality. Five lectures on mind, five on consciousness, and five on the functioning of the body were given.

Initiations were also conducted. Fransesca decorated the room where the classes were held. An angel, Master Jesus and hundreds of flowers were all dipped in glow paint including one hundred and fifty stars that hung from the ceiling. The room was in total darkness except for all the glowing objects. Five nights per topic were spent in class time.

Each class consisted of handouts and when necessary, diagrams:

> We are concerned with soul's realizations – in their objectifications on the mortal plane...The Cosmic conditions cannot be placed into shapes, objects, forms, boxes, patterns, from (such is known objectively – since they are FORMLESS in their unmanifests). They only become 'formed' when they assume the condition of matter. The unmanifest must eventually come into the manifested

condition and this is merely the second stage of Being! Its primordial condition is Cosmic!

Mortally, one may conceive of one's beginning as that moment when one becomes a living soul – yet in reality that is NOT one's 'beginning' for from the unformed you become the FORMED! That which is body is not the real "I" or soul's personality. It is only body, the vehicle of the soul! This is one's manifest!

Think what a gift it is to be alive! The joy of knowing what you are, who you are. Is it not a thrill to realize that as one breathes that one shares with every other living thing – every creature – every beauty – every personality – every mind – every other soul? Isn't it wonderful to realize that the elements, atoms and electrons through the universe are just waiting for you so that they may unite and form within you? Are you the right polarity? Isn't it wonderful to contemplate that you are a magnet? Isn't it wonderful to realize that you also 'give off' the flaming segments of life – when you touch another? Isn't it WONDERFUL to know that as one 'loves' one is able to do so because of the atoms of which one is composed? Isn't it wonderful to realize that elements have a weight and vibration and are polarized – so that they are attracted or repulsed? Is this not a 'human quality'? Can one see them as ENTITIES miniature representatives of God? He sent them forth to DO – and because they are acting and moving – they DO! Just think, in their very 'doing' you had the opportunity to become!

> It is because of this (in the holiest of all loves) that one is sitting and reading, without the action and attraction of atoms and their elements one would still be an unmanifested atom!

Fransesca became a spiritual mother to some of her students. Others filled empty places as she experienced emptiness when someone walked out of her heart. It was a priority for Fransesca to become a Christ person and to teach this path to others. As a Christ person it was important for her to remember the thoughtfulness of others.

In November 1961, Fransesca wrote (channeled by her Master A.) "The Rebirth of Miss Seedlet, The Beautiful."

MISS SEEDLET...The Beautiful

A tiny spark of Tree Life, caressed by Angel Breath, hesitated for an instant in space. It paused in cycle of Time, whirled about in its Cradle and cascaded to earth!

Tiny Miss Seedlet waved to her Companion Seed as they sped towards Nature's nesting Ground. Miniature seedlets snuggled cozily in fertile soil of Mother earth, drinking her gentle dew greedily. Warm spring sun blessed their delicate seed forms with Love. Miss Seedlet's heart throbbed with joy – for she would soon see her Companion as he unfolded – then they would whisper sweet thoughts from the bosom of Mother Earth. Ultimately they awakened from their slumber in earth's nesting bed!

Proudly they rustled their first tiny branches, saying, "We are born again! How good it is to breathe and love once more!"

Throbbing with new life they excelled themselves, and grew...and...grew...and grew! Shy Miss Seedlet blushed prettily when hoardes of Princely Bees hummed through her leaflets powdering the Bridal Garment with her Companions' pollen. Her Virgin Veil of Spring blossoms – blessed by his ardor – perfumed the valley with a heavenly scent, and pastel petals of New Love, in a bridal carpet fluttered at her feet.

Handsome Male Companion shook himself vigorously – broadcasting his pollen far and wide, his blossoms remaining long after his beautiful lady was delivered of her fruit. He struggled mightily to protect Her – throwing out robust branches to safeguard the Fruit of His Young Bride. They gloried in their Springtime of Love, showering the Land with their essence. Creation the Wondrous!!

Twilight months neared, matured. Mrs. Seedlet wearied by the great weight upon her shoulders, drooped and weakened. In waning days of twilight her handsome male Companion whispered brave encouragement. "Beloved! Weep not...a Long Winter Night is upon us, and we are no longer young and fruitful, but we shall return!! Our blossoms have born much fruit and produced rich seed, thus through this we shall live again, – and the memory of our Love is everywhere. Our roots lie deep in Natures' womb and together we shall rest there in our Long Sleep, but return to another rebirth. It is NOT farewell, Beautiful Lady, be comforted."

Although the sting of Autumn's Frost was deep in her tired veins, Quivering Lady blew – a kiss towards him. Trembling with cold, handsome Companion grasped her russet leaf as it touched him, holding it firmly against his breast. She had understood his message, as her golden kiss of love testified. This was their final embrace in this era of Life!!!!!!

Winter winds whistled through their gnarled branches while saucy snowflakes crowned them with their Father's Love.

Tenderly God called them to His Bosom where they slept. He smiled upon his handiwork, musing within Himself that soon he would awaken them again, – when Mother Earth had readied the Cradle for their rebirth!! All was well!

Resurrection would come for them again – and again – and again until they had made perfect seed out of His image!

Mrs. Seedlet, the Beautiful and Handsome Male slept in sweet peace!

The moral: Life's Lessons: Sharing – giving – seeding – planting-

Causing – affecting – flowering – maturing –aging – dying-to-earth –

Awakening to birth – resting and contemplating on Life's Lessons –

Waiting for birth again.

The Question – Is ReBirth Fact or Fiction?

God's Law is immutable!!! And is identical in all Kingdoms. There would be chaos in Cosmic rhythm if birth, re-birth, transition and change were only available to the Lesser – while being exempt for the Greater Kingdoms – in and through the Kingdom of Man!

Observe Nature in all Kingdoms if you would see the continuity of all life, in its eternal struggle to be what it had come to express. Each-Seedlet-of-Soul strives for that perfection state, its ideal out of every facet of itself.

Mother Earth in the Flower of Spring, through sap of life, births each soul – seedlet as it lives, learns, yearns and loves.

Father Wisdom calls it home for a time of Rest and Preparation. Seedlet planted its groundwork, scattering its pattern far and wide, and It yearns to return to see the effects for which it alone was responsible! Soul speaks eternally. "I came as cause and since my fruits or their seeds were imperfect, I MUST return again!"

Father Wisdom replies, "Yes, this you shall do – but now you are weary and must rest, while you recapitulate your soul's endeavours. I draw my Blanket of Sleep about you, while you come to Me for a time, then later, when you have studied and reflected, I shall return you to Mother Earth once more, where you shall witness the Offsprings of your soul's efforts.

So endeth the lesson.

One can see the love and respect for nature and for the cycles of life in this story.

Chapter Four

San Jose

Fransesca's Master dictated "A Treatise" (Appendix ll) consisting of five sections: concentration, meditation, rhythmic breathing, contemplation and Samadhi-ecstasy were the subjects. Fransesca underwent the study of all that was described. The purpose of the Treatise is for soul realization.

In thirty-six years Fransesca proved that "Love from the Divine Plane – and union with the personal Master is indeed the Pearl without Price." The ultimate dedication for Fransesca was serving her personal master and being a channel. She wrote:

> This union and sacred trust as his Channel is not captured in a moment; nor through a few years of happen stance regimentation or meditation! Union of Soul to Soul – Mind to Mind – consciousness into consciousness comes about only through DEDICATION and ABSOLUTE obedience! They have revealed that service and devoted attention – through obedience – with love and Master manifestation as the motive, ARE the requisites for Master Channeling!

Therefore, channeling is a life of dedication – service and is Love's reward on the highest plane. It can never be on a mortal plane, since it is Cosmic Union with the Beloved!

A disciple is chosen because they love and wish to manifest for him – to benefit others besides themselves! Secondly they are chosen because of willingness to adapt themselves to a regulated regime of preparation and obedience. Thirdly, the motive which inspires them indicates their goal and if this is one of universality – or sharing the Master's love – then the chances are good that they will receive this treasured Cosmic guidance and instruction.

Our mission is to instill higher goals and precepts in others in order that they too might become Channels for words of Light and in Ways of Love!

While the relationship is one of the invisible with the visible – the personal relationship is of such soul stirring qualities.

To be touched by the Presence of Master T and the Shining Soul is a wondrous experience as they are existent in every shade of FEELING!

The moments with the Master are all spent in serious study and questions, for all details of my personal life are discussed with him.

Fransesca devoted seventeen hours a day to spiritual work while living in San Jose.

Fransesca wrote "Words from the Masters" as channeled by her Master. It was distributed to class members and published in a monthly newsletter:

Words From The Masters

Love and Doubt:

When you live in Love, you believe, and all is bright for you.
By this you will know that you are in the WORLD OF LOVE.
There is no doubt there.
As soon as you begin to doubt, it shows that Love is absent.

As soon as the disciple definitely starts on the Way, great hardships will appear which may cause him to stumble.
He should not be disturbed by them, nor led astray by them.
To be reconciled to God is to accept His Love.

Weeping:

The disciple should weep when no one is watching him. Then weeping is a blessing. He can weep before others about human affairs, but when he is weeping about something DIVINE, he should weep by himself.

When some Divine blessing cannot be poured out upon the disciple,
The cause is NOT IN GOD – BUT IN THE DISCIPLE!!!!
God has prepared a blessing for everyone.

The disciple lives on the earth but thinks about heaven.
He works for the REALIZATION of the Divine laws on earth.

ENDURE ALL for the sake of Love until you attain Love.
When it comes you will receive patience – PATIENCE!!!!!!!

Only LOVE teaches OBEDIENCE.
The new obedience is obedience OUT OF LOVE.
"He who loves Me will keep my commandments."
This is possible only with Love and then comes the gift; "And I shall abide with you, even unto the end of the world."

Obedience and Learning

When the disciple receives the Love of His Master, he is obedient, so that Love may be planted in him. But he learns in order that Love may grow in him!!!!

The Hands:

The hands were created for work.
When the disciple looks on them, they say,
"We were created for work!"
The disciple MUST NOT BE INDOLENT!!!!!!!!

His Look:

The look of the eyes should be soft and pure, concentrated and always in contact with some Divine Thought.

The look of the disciple is such that it NEVER disturbs the harmony in others.
The best greeting is that OF THE EYES. It is the purest and God accepts it.
Love is something spiritual and Divine.
It finds expression in the physical world through the eyes.

Posture of the Disciple:

The disciple must always have an erect posture. It keeps his consciousness awake and predisposes his Spirit to work.

Clothing:

The disciple is careful of his clothes because they
Are impregnated with his own aura. His clothing must be loose and comfortable.
NOT THE CLOTHES – but the FACE should stand out!!!
And not the face – BUT THE SOUL!!!!

The hands of a disciple must always be of a moderate temperature.
They must be warm.
Cold hands indicate an oppressed mind.
More sunshine is necessary. Warmth brings wellbeing of spirit.

Money:

The disciple should keep the following rule in their relations:
SERVICE – for SERVICE.
Money can spoil a man. It bears ANOTHERS' IMAGE – while SERVICE
bears the image of Love. Through Service the disciple receives and delivers the IMAGE OF LOVE.
The disciple must serve only OUT OF LOVE.
The disciple should never ASK for money.
He should DO something to EARN THE MONEY.
The disciple must always SERVE – and <u>then</u> RECEIVE.
but NEVER receive – WITHOUT – serving!!

Companionship:

The disciple should associate with people more advanced than himself, in order to learn from them.
He should also associate with men of his level, who would encourage him and make him more zealous in his work.
He must also descend to those of a lower level than he in order to HELP THEM.
If he gives his support to men lower than he is, beings of a HIGHER ORDER will support him.

Suffering:

The disciple must face suffering with joy – for he will LEARN something good from it.
If he understands suffering thus – he will grow young.
Humanity passes through the region of suffering during only one phase of its development.
Suffering prepares the nervous system to endure a new LIGHT which will come.

Fransesca's prayer is that the reader will find "Him within yourself or at your side and be glorified in the peace which this union brings." She finds Him related in herself and with all things, all souls. This was an exhilarating experience.

Fransesca wrote "Once Upon A time: Soul's Temple Cloth" in November 1961 as an allegory. The story covers several lessons and is an inspired piece of writing. Christ taught in parables:

"The Master knew the heart of His followers – who as 'little children' heard His words, according to their own need and desires. He was a past Master in unfolding His message within the lines of parables."

Once Upon A Time: Souls' Temple Cloth

Little Soul danced towards the Shining Light when Heavens' grapevine heralded the Good News that God had summoned Her to His footstool. She clapped her tiny hands, flitting through airy spheres like thistle down. She was going to Another Home!!! Another Home!!! oh my! how exciting!!!

Iridescent strands of Light wound together in intricate pattern formed the pathway to her Father's Gate...and Little Soul knelt sweetly before she crosses the Beam of Love to His Heart. One spidery thread of luminous Light touched her as she rose and stood before her God.

"Oh my!" she thought, "I cannot see His Face, just like They have said, but I feel His presence everywhere, and My Soul is nearly bursting!!! It will be difficult to leave This World, – so filled with love – but I shan't forget what I have learned." Fluttering with eagerness, she sped toward Him and the Spirit of God enfolded her.

"So my Child – you wish to leave Us and return to earth?" The SOUND of His Voice quickened her spirit, as she cupped her tiny face in her hands. "Yes, my Father, if you would have me go, I will do my best to abide by that which I have been taught here, during my Rest Period in Realm of Soul."

The little heart within her cosmic breast beat wildly as the Spirit of God embraced her. "Tiny One, – thou art eager – and it is well that thou goeth forth to live again. Thy hour hath come to experience, – for thou hast learnt thy lessons of Life well. See therefore, that in thy return thou heedeth all which Thou has been taught, during thy Cycle with Us." "Oh, my Father, I will!!!...I will!!! I shall be ever so good, – and kind and true, and I shall NEVER forget all "They" have taught me – I have learnt each Lesson and shall remember to always be my Father's Child." His smile of endearment touched her with rapture, and once again tiny hands covered her angelic face and she wept.

The Spirit of God moved through her, and Little Soul was freed for her return to earth.

As she left Realm of Soul – God Essence wrapped itself about her, clinging to her diaphanous form. A silken thread extended Itself, its' Cause lying in the Heart of God. She touched the silken cord smiling contentedly, "I am always joined to My Father by this thread – isn't it wonderful?" Other Little Souls awaiting their hour for re-birth smiled with her as they paused in their movement through His hallowed Arc.

She descended!

Little Soul left God's Home, shiny and bright, drifting to earth on Star beams, light as a feather and overflowing with love. Her Golden Temple Cloth was the Magic Carpet which whisked her towards a hungry mother heart below.

She mused: 'Yes, there She is – MY mother!!!! She is more beautiful than I pictured...but oh...she is SO lonely...she has waited for me for such a long, long time, but I couldn't come any sooner, as it was not Our Time. My beautiful mother ...how exhausted she is, yet so brave. Now, – I see my Father, he is waiting for Me too. I hope he will be happy that I am a Girl, for I know Mother wants ME! It pains me to see her suffering, but yet, I must wait until the Hour has come for my earthly birth. I can see my Form in her and it is just like I had pictured, we shall be ONE when my Soul comes into life's stream again!

Little Soul hovered near her parents patiently...and at the precise moment destined for her – she was a Living Soul through the Breath of Life! The Temple Cloth in which God had sent her forth, nestled gently into the small form, blending Itself in the atoms and fibres of her Being. She was Living Life again – and the Love life of her new sphere began. "What rapture!" Thought Little Soul!

She grew – and grew – and grew – while her Golden Temple Cloth altered, taking on other colors, as she began to live and do! Her Temple Cloth lost some of its luster through the years, when sorrowful things, or bad deeds and thoughts stained Its' Cloth. Fluttering bravely inside Its Temple, soul tried again and again to renovate Its' Garment, and remodel it as a fitting Robe for Its' Lord to see.

"Ah!:" It sighed, "here is a rent in my garment – where I weakened and fell into Temptation. My God – I pray for Thy forgiveness – help me to mend this tear." God was gracious and good, and forgave His child – for indeed she was of Him...Living Soul.

Alas, Little Soul forgot again – and again – and again – growing into maturity with fretfulness in increased activity. God spoke, "Child! Child!! Heed Me! I sent thee forth shrouded in My Temple Cloth, pure and golden and Thou hast worn It, using it unwisely, disregarding My counsel. Thy Cloth art weakened, yeah in portions it art threadbare, – soon it shall cover Thee not, and Thy Soul will drift away without Its' Garment." "But Father," Little Soul replied "You gave it to me to wear when I came to earth. It is mine to use. When I have used it up, you will give me another one, won't You?"

God sighed deeply.

"Nay Child, I give thee none other. Thy Temple Cloth, in which I tenderly wrapped thee as Living Soul art for one lifetime only – it is NOT thine – but it art Mine. Thy Garment of flesh art of all My kingdoms, elements and principals. It shall be returned to Me in virgin forms, as It wert given Thee." Soul covered her face once more, ashamed. "I allotted thee – Measure of Golden Cloth, whose woof and warp art of My Life, each thread thereof blended in Light of My Life, and Love of My Heart. Each jot and title belongeth to Me! If thou useth thy portion, or desecrated it before Thy time art spent, thou hast destroyed My Temple Cloth – which I loaned thee. When Thy Soul returneth to Me, it will be saddened by thy wastefulness, for Thy Temple Cloth art impressed with the spoils of thy extravagances of MY Living Life!"

Poor Little Soul bowed in humility. "Yes, Lord, – my God, I shall honour my Temple Garment, more circumspectively hereafter." He smiled – when Little Soul repented.

The Golden Temple Cloth, in which Little Soul was enshrouded, quivered in agitation, while flickering Light danced from Its' form. God had spoken! And the altar in Souls' heart burnt brightly again, as His Temple Cloth fell gracefully about Its form.

Christ Within was pleased.

Chapter Five

San Jose

Fransesca typed all her inspirational material. This included dictations by her personal Master, meditations and communion discussions. She was a clear channel for the teachings of certain Masters and served the Christ. She believed that we are all united through love and that God's image becomes our image and our love.

The following are Fransesca's notes taken from lectures given to class members on May 8 and May 15, 1963 by Master J. and Master T.

> Only segment of consciousness is in the body – the cosmic counterpart (or cosmic consciousness) is the goal.
>
> Mind is the power which MOVES – whilst 'consciousness' waits (or hovers) waiting for the 'thought of mind.' Realizations are brought into thought extensions of this small segment of consciousness.

If man relied upon this segment of consciousness he would be unable to realize anything outside of himself or the world in which he lives.

Limited perception of the ego is a NOTHING in its finiteness – in comparison to the infinite expansion of non limitation.

You shall not sit and wait for mind and its companion consciousness to come to you – you must reach out to it, thereby expanding your consciousness and becoming a greater force field.

Body has the segment of mind and consciousness. Form is not limited since it is immaterial. Body is material – limited in its 2 – D function and three dimensional expression. Conscious and subjective mind rely upon the five senses – always THROUGH the body.

Mental form has its first manifestations through form, not body. The aura is man's consciousness – his force field. In extension, the force field expands and his form enlarges and grows.

Mind is the mover, whilst consciousness is the translator of the message of mind.

Mortal segment therefore expands by the higher form of mind through its translations.

Man can only respond in five manners in his body because he has only five perceptive centres.

Consciousness waits in the 'hovering condition' to receive the thoughts as it translates the thought of mind the mover – it moves with vibrations and body responds to its impulses.

Touching spiritual form with its consciousness – then and only then (for the first time) man begins to feel responding to Infinite Impulses which have no corresponding stimuli in the five physical senses. This is the first awakening of the soul eye in man – the sixth sense. Light dawns. First enlightenment!

Mental form is the bridge which carries man over into Infinite conditions. From here on it is fourth dimensional and fifth, sixth and seventh.

Man must go beyond the third dimensional aspect in order to enlarge his aura – force field, otherwise he remains four squared, boxed, imprisoned. Fourth dimension brings fullness, magnetic aura and warmth.

Consciousness lies hovering as it translates the mortal thought interpreting it only according to its ability to do so.

Mind is positive. If consciousness is so positive, it translates according to its own desires and personal ought, the will of the body (mind) will prevail and 'so be it' to each man. Consciousness is the passive quality and must ever be the Receiver!

"Two hundred and eighty-seven seekers passed through our doors until the Master weeded them out to the eighteen for deep and private study." The classes from then on consisted of eighteen students.

Fransesca also typed and recorded life cycles initially free of charge and later for a fee. She had an excellent attunement with her Master.

After her son died, Fransesca often wished for another child. She was advised in a meditation that people in the world were there for her to love. This is how people became her love and life.

> I gave up my diary writing because the world was "adopted" As my children, sisters, families, etc. Then the spiritual life – church, doing for others filled a vital spot but always was the child need of that special dream daughter. I filled it. (1946). The Cosmic finally got through to me that the WORLD was to be my mothering place – that the wee souls with their problems, growths, needs were to become my place to serve them and love them. All of a sudden I had children everywhere.
>
> Then came the big joy of realizing something very powerfully, what tremendous effect my mama's and papa's words, training, etc. had affected me and I prayed if only I could be like my mama, not so serious like papa. And lo, I am a combination of both of them and so I have 'mama'd' lots of children in many places.

In a letter to Irene written on December 26, 1960 Fransesca wrote about becoming like a small child:

> In our fullness we realize then that this little child truly is closer to God through all the rest of their life – and this is the kind of 'little child' who must come into the Kingdom. When the material is 'nothing,' when the problems of life are 'as nothing' when only the DAY BEFORE us is wonderful, thrilling, exciting, beautiful, living, adoring – when Christ in us is a little baby and we are that little baby and He is living in us and we are HE! And it is so nice and so comforting to know this "as a little child."

Fransesca kept and trained cockatiels. She wrote about them in an article, "The Miracle of Birth." A young cockatiel needed parenting as it was abandoned. Fransesca placed this little bird in a cloth bag tied around her neck and kept shifts to feed it every few hours. Her devotion extended to other animals on many occasions.

Fransesca had several people in San Jose with whom she had developed close and loving relationships. Fransesca met Ken from Toronto, Canada when he visited her in San Jose. At the time, Fransesca was sixty years old. A courtship followed and she and Ken eventually married. Fransesca then relocated to Toronto.

In 1966 Fransesca visited San Jose for six weeks. She stayed in a furnished, rented apartment. Class members added throw rugs and flowers. Her husband came for twelve days but then returned to Toronto. They rented a car for one week and did sightseeing where they also visited San Fransisco and went to Fisherman's Wharf. The alone time away from home that Fransesca and Ken had together was like a belated honeymoon. She and Ken investigated the possibility of relocating to San Jose.

Fransesca held two classes a week as well as gave consultations daily. She had a large wall chart to schedule consultations, appointments and visits. Some of the class members drove long distances to attend the classes. It was a joy filled time and a family feeling dominated within everyone. All "gave beautifully" and were happy to be together again. They also had an open house for friends, husbands and wives. The private portion was restricted to eighteen members, those who had initially been in the closed classes.

Fransesca was showered with love, goodness and sharing. All was harmonious and flowed smoothly. "Very good to be at home to the children of the flock. All the kids came home for Mama." Fransesca was called "Mama" by her students. She completed a seven-year cycle in San Jose.

Fransesca always said, "Thy will always. The Masters always know best." The kind of Cosmic Love that the Masters gave was unique. For class members, this experience with Mama would not come again in their lifetime.

On her way back to Toronto, Fransesca visited Irene in Seattle for three and a half days. They maintained a long correspondence with one another. The connection between them involved past lives. It was a wonderful relaxing time spent with Irene and her husband. Irene said, "A little piece of me is always with someone I love...and a little piece of them is with me."

Fransesca's students also gifted her with travel to Lake Louise and Vancouver.

Upon her return to Toronto, Fransesca thanked the class members by letter, which she called a "memory book." It was written with deep love and gratitude for all the camaraderie, kinship and joy she shared during her visit to San Jose and so that others could have memories after Fransesca left. The classes continued through tape recordings.

On September 5, 1967 Fransesca conducted a memorial service for her special spiritual daughter Irene who passed away from cancer. It was a moving and beautiful service.

Fransesca considered the years in San Jose to be her happiest. It was a time of teaching and consultations when Fransesca was most active spiritually. "Is there greater love than this for the love of One's Master – and obedient discipleship? Is this not the love for Brother and Sisters? This is true love!"

Her Master, A. wrote the following version of "The Beatitudes" Fransesca channeled the prayer.

Blessed are they who give – for of such is the Kingdom of God.

Blessed are the peacemakers – for in them lieth the soul and the wisdom of the Kingdom of God.

Blessed are the joyful – for in them reigneth the Joy of God within.

Blessed are they who seek after knowledge, for in them lieth the thirst to know Him and be unto His likeness.

Blessed are the lowly and forgiving in heart – for they traveleth the paths of Jesus of Nazarene, unto such, cometh joy of love's unbounding.

Blessed are they who faileth not to seek always the HEIGHTS of the animal kingdom; above – beyond – close by – IN ALL THINGS wherein lieth the Truth and the Light.

Blessed in them that hath – and giveth – the assurance of Life everlasting. Life beyond – which followeth as surely as night followeth after Day.

Most blessed is one – which upon arising, can KNOW – that in the hours of slumber – the soul hath rejoiced – and refreshed itself in the arms of the Loved Angels of God – and be blessed by ties in realms celestial. Oh, blessed indeed is such who partaketh – who giveth – who shareth – who, upon sharing likeso forgiveth from the heart – deeply and from within.

These are blessed beyond the words of mouth of mortal man, or the call only out of the lips – when with love

> overflowing, they can say "Father I forgive them. I ask forgiveness of me thy child.
>
> Make me understand in faith, unbounded in love, joyous in heart, that my joy from the night I share with all.

Fransesca's devotion and dedication were exceptional. Spiritual discipline took priority over everything else. The love of the Masters burned within her heart and soul. Her life was a beautiful example of a life lived with love.

Master T. suggested a technique for bringing comfort to oneself. The Master dictated:

> When one is sad, lonely, ill or distressed, imagine that in the centre of your heart a small figure of the Master is seated. Place your hand upon the heart, as though you were knocking on the door, waiting for Him to step forth, observe as He rises and comes out of the doorway of your heart to greet you. See Him as "living" and moving through your body – from the centre of your heart. Speak with Him asking Him to bless your heart, and you. Realize this – observing then as He blesses each part of your body. Be joyous with Him – be HAPPY as you feel this closeness with Him. Know that he is always there – that unconscious Master you need. Touch the doorway of your heart and say, "Master I need the comfort of your presence, please let me talk with you. Walk with me!" He is everywhere at once – His power is Love – which can correct all conditions. Only you and the Master within can commune together alone – like unto none other. He will ALWAYS be in the pillow of your heart – call upon Him, so He will be everywhere. Everywhere and watchful. "Ask and you shall

> receive." – knock and it shall be opened unto you." He is there! For He is Thee!" Don't separate yourself from Him, for the Master is nowhere else – but within your heart.

Someone once asked Fransesca why she was so intense about everything. She was also asked why everything was so important. She was questioned, "Why can't you find out about your body, mind and consciousness in books?" and "Why must you always 'make it real' to yourself? Isn't this a lot of work...is it worth all that trouble? Why do you bother?"

Fransesca replied, "Personal information is a joy and a privilege which cannot be compared to any mortal condition." Fransesca attends the Cosmic University where her Master is the Dean. He demands complete obedience and regular attendance in the schoolroom: "It is wonderful to be taught – through ONE who introduces other Masters to me for the furtherance of my education."

"It is worthwhile. It is important. It is worth every moment spent in yearning for ultimate union with God soul – for IDENTIFICATION. He lives. He lives in me. He is! He is! And I am THAT."

Chapter Six

Toronto

From 1964 to 1981, Fransesca lived in Toronto. From 1978 to 1981, I was privileged to be a student of hers for three and a half years.

Fransesca selected copies and excerpts of meditations and communion periods to share with me. Included also were notes taken from my calls to her as well as from visits to her home. When Fransesca came to live in Toronto she moved to Ken's house in a suburb in the northern part of the city. Ken had a son and a daughter. The son used fiberglass to work on dune buggies in the basement. The fumes made it difficult for Fransesca so Ken asked his son to stop this project. His request, however, was ignored.

Whenever there were family gatherings for picnics or holiday celebrations, Fransesca always wrote a thank you letter to all who attended. She also wrote an annual general letter to friends, family and acquaintances. The tone was always loving.

Fransesca was a homemaker and cooked Ken's meals. She said that Ken was "spoiled." Ken was a pharmacist and worked long shifts, many times coming home after eight or nine at night. Due to his hours Fransesca spent many hours alone.

In the beginning Fransesca had her meditation area in the basement. After the stepchildren moved out, the meditation room was transferred to the second floor. In her later years, Fransesca held her communion periods in the living room.

Fransesca and Ken created "flo-light" creations consisting primarily of jewellery such as earrings and pendants. They also made lamps, pyramids and pen sets. Layers of plexiglass were painted in purple, apricot, turquoise, emerald green, cherry red, blue, lime green and fuscia. They were a reflecting medium and highly charged and energized. No two pendants were alike for each was unique. The "flo-lights" were sold from their home and at bazaars. This workshop was in the basement.

Fransesca had two birds: an African parrot named Tutu and a Senegal named Happy Boy. They were house trained and sat on perches in the living room. At night they slept in their respective cages.

During my visits with Fransesca, she recounted parts of her life. I always left with a feeling of joy and upliftment. There was always a lot to share and to talk about.

Fransesca mentioned that Christmas was a sad time for her, because December 30th was the anniversary of her son's passing, as well as that of her brother-in-law's. Also, January 3rd marked the anniversary of her Poppa's passing.

Fransesca talked about many spiritual subjects. One of our first conversations dealt with Cosmic experience. She explained that true Cosmic experience is when one sees, hears and feels in all directions. The psychic self separates itself from the physical (astral). The body isn't felt and one knows oneself as consciousness. Fransesca also said that many people stop at the psychic level and do not go beyond to the spiritual.

Fransesca felt ashamed if she could not come to the Cosmic feeling happy and good. Feeling worthy of the Cosmic was important for her and she considered being worthy a sacred duty.

In a letter written to a friend in March 24, 1975 Fransesca wrote this excerpt which was given to a class in San Jose originally and was subsequently shared in letters:

> It isn't WHAT you know – but what you DO with what you know which is recognized by the Cosmic!
>
> It isn't WHO you are, but HOW you are, which is recognized by the Cosmic!
>
> It isn't what you HAVE but what you DO with what you have, which is recognized by the Cosmic!
>
> It isn't how much you received – but what you can GIVE, which is recognized by the Cosmic!

The following inspirational selection was also included in the same correspondence:

> When a student has been taught and has heard and refuted the knowledge presented to him – he can NOT be excused for improper attitude – or for lack of endeavour in correcting flaws in personality structure.
>
> It is only when he DOES NOT KNOW – or has not been taught, that his actions are allowed a modicum of indulgence! We cannot be indulgent with students who KNOW!

In another letter to a friend on January 26, 1977, Fransesca stated that "my consciousness is 'feeling.' It FEELS the images of my mind. Then the images of my mind have the power – and my consciousness feels that power..."

In the summer of 1978, Fransesca shared a portion of a meditation with me. The meditation was held on January 19, 1977 and concerned Divine Mind. Whenever Fransesca faced a challenge, she would affirm, "Divine Mind in me. Let us do." Fransesca wrote:

> All is Mind. Everything which is of NOW is due to Great Divine Mind which moves through conscious mind. Fransesca retains a lot...for is part of memory cells – neurons which have become impressed themselves deeply as part of the subconscious and been brought out of the subjective state.
>
> Everything then, which is brought of or in a physical embodiment, is brought out through this same route. Subconscious to subjective state – to conscious mind – but the subjective state must be attained in order to tap the subconscious.
>
> What is there in the subconscious is what we put there. My personal subconscious is a 'strata' or level through which the universal subconscious moves...On the physical level, through the route of subconscious to conscious mind – the entity creates a mental image (or picture and 'sees' it in a certain 'form' because of the qualities which the entity responds to). The qualities are the PERSON!
>
> Whatever we see is what is in OUR mind...One sees that is in Mind, all that which is seen is! EXISTS!...Only that

> which comes through the subconscious via the subjective state to brain mind, can you say "I see." When in the state or condition of Cosmic consciousness all which you see – is because it is in Cosmic Mind. You have then tapped your own source of Cosmic consciousness and Its Mind.

All Fransesca's communions were spoken out loud and recorded until the last years of her life:

> ...in this verbal communion I name the POSITIVE manifestation whereas the silent communion is a negative. i.e. non-recorded. Sound is so important to me...All which is of the Cosmic Divine Mind is unmanifested until it is created in MATTER – then it becomes a manifest on the material plane (i.e. an unmanifest is a negative much like the negative in a camera until it is developed when it becomes a positive picture). Without words or sound Master T would be soundless and unmanifested or in a negative (inactive) state or condition...The unmanifested condition is then BEING searching for ITS self.

Fransesca kept up an avid correspondence with a several people. Most of what was written was spiritual in context. Fransesca appreciated responses to her letters and said "This is half of the sharing, isn't it – knowing what response comes from the other end."

"It was Cosmically necessary to complete those tasks we came here to do." Fransesca also said that she "accepted guidance and advice and counsel from anyone if they knew more about a subject than I do – and I am eager to learn. It does rub me the wrong way to be told what and how to do something that is all old stuff to me."

Her Master dictated:

"You are the mistress of the situation – mistress in your own home and capable of being mistress in any condition. I wish you always to take the first step, the first words, the first movement so that you remain in control of all situations."

During a visit with Fransesca a technique for meditation was described. This can also be found in the "Treatise" (see appendix). Fransesca taught meditation to her students in San Jose. She stressed to her students the importance of writing everything down. She explained:

> There were active and inactive phases of meditation. Let the thoughts to flow through. Release and let go of the negative thoughts. The thoughts will eventually peter out to a silent pause. Then there is a true form of deep communion. Find a special time each day. Realize that one cannot make one's mind a blank. Obey the guidance received. Write down the start and finish times. Allow one hour for meditation. One can sit and be alert. Listen carefully. A true meditative state is being mentally alert. One can become sensitive and more attuned to a much higher channel. One can find joy in absolute silence of thought. Then one is in a subjective state by being half way between being awake and being asleep. One is not awake to the conscious self.

In a letter dated April 5, 1978, Fransesca wrote about her sister Lu with whom she kept in close contact. Her sister loved humour so Fransesca sent her humourous quotes in letters. They also called one another on a regular basis.

Her Master guided Fransesca to write that, "Love begets love. Love is a powerful force. Cosmic love is man's strength. It is not his weakness."

Fransesca taught that God in each person is striving to become the Son, the Christ Spirit. The God within begets. Several of Fransesca's favourite hymns were "More Like the Master Would I Be" and "Christ Lives Today." She also said that the further one walks the Way, the more one is alone. Fransesca experienced feelings of loneliness.

Real love is eternal love. It is remembered again and again and again. The same feeling one has felt initially always comes back, explained Fransesca.

In a meditation held in February 1977, the theme was "Mind and Seeing." This was written about in a letter on July 17, 1978:

> All is mind. Divine mind moves through conscious mind from subconscious mind to subjective state to conscious mind. To tap the subconscious subjective state must be achieved. Universal subconscious moves through personal subconscious. One sees ALL that is in mind and all that which is seen is! EXISTS!
>
> Can say "I see" via the subjective mind to brain mind. When in cosmic consciousness – all that which is is in Cosmic mind. A person taps into their own source of Cosmic consciousness and its mind. All that which one is capable of seeing one will see.

On January 4, 1979 Fransesca spoke about Aquarian characteristics. She was an Aquarius with her birthday being on January 26. "Leadership is a trait. Other people resent 'leadership.' The present-day cliché of wanting 'to do my own thing' seems that everyone wants to do their own thing and in their own way. Therefore no one is really listening to the rest of the world, only to the direction they want to go."

Fransesca had methods to bring herself out in the open so that her Master self can rule, lead, teach and can in all eventuality be and become the whole self. She advised involving oneself in self-examination when an individual one loved or trusted drops out of one's life. She suggested:

> Remove oneself to a quiet place and ask oneself, 'was I at fault? Did I overstep my authority? What did I do or say? How did I act?' Sometimes we can be wrong. Sometimes when we talk about it with ourselves we notice something which had escaped us before – it DOES help us a great deal in further situations so we know how to handle them.

Jealousy also affects Aquarians. Fransesca tried very hard to never talk down to anyone. She tried to speak on the same level as another. She taught that doing so was the kind way:

> The hardest lesson for an Aquarian to conquer is the disciplining of energies, time, and priorities. Things we want to do and plan for. We bite off more than we can chew. We take on tasks. We say 'yes' when we should have said 'no.' We suffer health wise if we try to do it all. We know darn well we cannot, but conscious self which is sometimes a very stubborn creature says, 'I can do anything!'...Let us consider first what the priorities are. There are always certain things in our life which come first. That is the important area to start with. When we have done that, then we can tackle the smaller thing and the little things which we forgot to do because we're so busy.

Fransesca was a highly organized individual. She was also excellent with time management and accomplished many things in one day. She had a 'thing' about keeping one's word:

> "It is a real task master to me. This came from my own mama, poppa training. One did not just break their word, ever ever, unless they lost their mind. And now with deeper cosmic training, I surely wouldn't dare! People who don't keep their word don't know any better."

On January 8, 1979 Fransesca spoke to me about her son Roland. She thought of him as a Christ babe born to her. When she truly realized this, she cried and cried. Fransesca celebrated his fiftieth birthday on December 30, 1978.

When Fransesca prayed she held the first three fingers of each hand together in the shape of a triangle and placed it in front of the solar plexus. The thumb is positive, the index finger neutral and the third finger is negative in polarity.

In a letter written January 30, 1979 Fransesca wrote:

"Anything we love – we will have to labour with – otherwise we are not really caring."

And labour she did. Fransesca put energy into everything she accomplished. Her thoroughness was evident when having visitors to her home for "flo-light" purchases, sharing wholeheartedly with her students, sorting bird seed for Happy Boy and Tutu, in the preparation of meals, and corresponding with others. She was always giving and serving more than one hundred percent.

In a letter written to a student on January 31, 1979 Fransesca wrote about mediums and channels, a popular topic of the day:

> So we come to mediums of 'channels.' I use the term loosely momentarily and this thought of 'possession' – another body entering a mortal body and talking from it and through it, ruling the entire life, etc. Well hogwash, say we!

For one thing, only one soul can inhabit one body at one time. That's logic and I am logical in spite of all the higher attainment, desires and goals!

...There is no taking over by any entity either on the physical or cosmic plane! Then what possess us? Where do mediums (or others) get the idea of this influence? And how does it come about?

A discarnate can reach an individual on this plane of a mind-to-mind basis, through emotional impact. The conscious self receiving the impulse and retranslates that impulse (via the route of consciousness) according to <u>their</u> own interpretation of the impulse!

That is why I am so adamant about striving for the very highest so Fransesca's conscious self is not in the way – and the higher Self or Cosmic personality can interpret through its consciousness what the true meaning of the impulse is...I wish to be had by my true identity – inner self – Master self because of the following:

We are completely and totally motivated in our life, deeds and actions, on the 3D or physical plane by those things which we experience as an individual or an entity...

We come to realize that everything in our life has an impact, creating a series of small pictures or images in the neurons of our brain. Some are etched deeply, others very faintly. This is part of our subconscious level...

Now we are back to the channeling again. Those who function on the level of the 3D world – and are ruled by things of this world can only interpret according to their own evolvement! No lesser, no higher! They refer whether knowingly or unknowingly to their own reactions which are awakened in them...this is frequently the call as we see in others quite often a reflection of ourselves.

What is the method of channeling...Does it sound familiar? Have we those words before, is there something familiar about it – to us? Quite often it is. I do not say that the medium or channeling is false – or improper, because that person believes that this is the truth! And to those who haven't gone very far yet it appears to be truth! (in portions that is) for it is the net result of that person's life.

We are all actors and actresses in our own life – we 'play' a role (conscious self) but very few manifest the true role – the true self – as most are ruled by the subconscious nature – emotions, reactions and relive that drama over and over again in many forms, never totally dismissing the possession of themselves. When I was put on the testing block some 30 years ago, I was not permitted to read anything, nor to attend anything, nor to discuss anything with anyone! I spent many hours each day and night clearing my subconscious of the unwelcome intruders, replacing the unwelcome with the welcome ones.

I did not want to talk, teach or help others through my own picture images, my own personal subconscious reactions. I wanted something much higher...

You are only possessed by your thoughts!!! Or the thoughts of others which you have allowed yourself to be possessed by. Think of all the people you know who are possessed! Possessed by fears – insecure, inability to perform, afraid to speak, think, act or do! Fear of failure, inadequacies, health, fears of catching this, that or the other thing...These are their own possessors!

When we are able to rid ourselves of most of our junk thoughts and have faced them for what they are (the ogre in the closet of thoughts) we then begin to know ourselves...

In our world in which we live now – we are also living what we have been. We retain memories and it is through this Divine Channel in ourselves that Divine Mind functions.

Now this association is much different than on the 3D plane...Then out of my own sub and akashic subconscious strata some pictured thought comes to the screen of mind and I immediately assess this picture which has a meaning – a translation so to speak – and has a bearing on our conversation...

A beam of light (or energy) is directed to that area of my brain which contains all sorts of information and there is an immediate response in me of deep feeling (not emotion). It is as though a door opens and I look upon scenes of childhood – other lives or touch the love of some wondrous soul. It is total recall and for those moments I am AS ONE with Them – the thing or the condition on that same state of being. I feel the beauty of their personality and as this 'beam' is held the conversation is fluent. It is an immediate direct transference of the thought or subject, without hesitation...When we have channeled for those cosmic souls, there was never any gruesome aspect to my countenance. Not squirming. Only tremendous power, excitation, joy, love so overpowering the walls in our room seemed to push it back at all of us with a holy force! It could not be misconstrued by anyone. I would remember the first opening portion, the closing portion but what was in between was like a 'dream' and thankfully the tape recorders were always running.

Fransesca taught that it was important to love the Self:

The Inner Self is fearless. The Inner Self exists on the Divine plane of the body. The inner self is emotionless, the inner self is Divine feeling without mortal emotions.

The projection of the Divine Self is beauty, joy, peace; contentment, tenderness, sweetness, ideas – courage, stamina, conquests, devotion, dedication are all of the Divine World.

Fransesca advised to, "Assume a lovely sharing with a companion – one's own Divine self."

Fransesca recorded the chanelling sessions during the classes held in San Jose.

Chapter Seven

Toronto

Fransesca had great respect for natural law: "Everything must be a natural law. Whenever we overdo anything...no matter what it may be we are not following natural law and in our way of life with thoughts, actions, etc. Our body thus reacts to this punishment we have given ourselves."

Fransesca was also blessed with a common sense that was highly developed. She also had a strong desire that no one was going to fool her. In addition, she was determined that "it must be right" or she would not have any part in something.

She taught that one is to "accept being happy, peaceful and filled with expectation" daily because it is a good way to start one's day.

When someone needed her, Fransesca put aside her aches as well as her feelings. People were in her life for her to give and to serve. For twenty-seven years Fransesca served for free. She was not allowed to charge fees until later in life. She explained that "one can serve others by kindness, thoughtfulness, doing something for someone which they might not be able to do for themselves at certain times in their life."

Much of Fransesca's service was through correspondence. In 1979 she typed 17,750 words in letters in one week. When typing, she used earplugs and closed her eyes.

When asked whether one is tested by the Cosmic, Fransesca explained:

> Tests are put in our path, not on purpose but because we are worthy of them so that we can draw upon inner knowledge, attunement, etc. and thus prove them out for ourselves. If everything went along lovingly, beautifully, excitedly and 'high-rise' all the time, we would learn exactly nothing and would have no need for being here...we grow, evolve, through experience and nothing else. We may become intelligent through books, reading etc. but we only KNOW through our realization and thus do we find truths!

In one of Fransesca's communion meditations she described what these periods involved:

> I cannot properly call them 'meditations' as most people speak of it, for they are communications, discussions, instructions and much love flowing, humour, tears and moments of ecstasy...After so many long years in this form of reception, I am 100% aware of Their presence(s), also of approval or that I am not understanding the subject as clearly as They would desire. There is hesitancy around me, as though there is a slow down of energies, or giving me an opportunity to rephrase my thought, so that it coincides with Theirs. When this attunement is established and I am receiving as They would have me do, the flow is just beautiful. It is very difficult to explain unless a tape (or many) have been heard...

> It is not easy to compare something in the Cosmic sense, which has no objective things in it and I am usually asking for a 'picture' something by which I can compare in relationship to physical things, which clarifies the subject much more easily...Another thing which is common in our communications, is that I try to keep things IMPERSONAL – as possible. If there is a reference to some individual they usually become a number (or letter of the alphabet). This assists me in removing them from my mind and causing something to be Impersonal so I can handle the subject in a much better manner.

> Realization is a Cosmic sensation. Then realization as a Cosmic sensation is the realization in a Cosmic state of consciousness!

Fransesca was grateful that she had a close friend with whom she could share. She also had several students with whom she maintained a close connection. It meant a lot to her to communicate spiritually and to have the opportunity to talk about little things, like pets, humour and daily living. She explained that "the beauty of any relationship when everything seems to fall in place as a natural Oneness."

> Love is a powerful energy...love impresses the self, in form, for love is a form of its consciousness which is in levels, degrees of energy. We can form it and do in physical, spiritual, all inclusive, personal and impersonal manner and in universal manner...The Divine form manifesting on earth impresses itself through a channel, so others would feel the impact of this love energy...This love energy is not only felt but it can be observed...

On June 12, 1979 Fransesca had a meditation regarding her being a channel for the Masters T. This was originally discussed on December 18, 1977. Fransesca kept a meditation book over the years in which she transcribed her meditations. They consisted of notes taken from tapes channeled for Master T.

In a meditation on June 20, 1979 Fransesca discussed the word "form" and its meaning:

> I also separate the word form – as a f-o-r-m – is not indicative of a shape – but a 'forming' which we do with our mind and consciousness, and all of us do not 'form' things in the same manner. The word is used quite frequently when we associate it with consciousness and how we are 'forming' our way of life – ideations, thoughts, etc. e.g. A thought of anger in one individual would create a 'form' according to their emotions and one who could 'see' or perceive through feelings this 'form' might see it as red dagger flashes in the aura – another might 'see' it or feel it as flames – heat, etc. and this become the 'formings' of our nature personal to each one.

Form then, as Fransesca meant it, is not physical. It is a "thing" of one's consciousness:

> All forms are concepts, ideals, beliefs, convictions, truths to us as we might have known them so we FORM them. We are playmates in when we are young...so our playmate in our infancy has some 'form' to us – invisible to anyone else usually and the children only tell someone else about it according to their ability to convey or describe the 'form.' FORMS are the result of our consciousness – our evaluation – from an emotional or soul plane.

Franseseca received a teaching about formings.

One needs to be careful of how we 'form' for WE ARE THE CREATOR OF THESE FORMINGS. The formings live in our world, in our magnetic field, in our aura – and others are touched and moved by them or are rejected by them. It really goes back to "beauty is in the eyes of the beholder? And we BEHOLD things in our world and the world about us and within us.

In a letter written to a friend on August 11, 1979, Fransesca mentioned her love of pets. When something is wrong with them, she was "more torn apart" than when something was wrong with herself.

...because I figured that humans could ALWAYS tell where it hurt – why – so that we could DO something about it. But our pets can only give us that sorrowful eye – or droopy feathers – or dropped tail – and we wonder – WHAT can I DO? And the "DO" question is the hardest to bear.

Love is the GREATEST HEALING QUALITY and power there is. This is CHRIST like service. There is nothing to compare it to or by...He was just there! – ready – willing. Giving HIS knowledge, sharing, loving, serving, as a son of God (Jesus).

...I realize as we talk to people who come here – we give them our cosmic picture – lessons and stories, which they respond to and they always feel the radiations of love-energy which impresses the 'picture stories' indelibly in memory. And 99 times out of a hundred they leave here greatly uplifted. They also carry the 'pictured' messages

> and lessons as a memory, so the love lives on and on, as a radiation, an emanation and Cosmic energy all of which is healing in its highest form.

Fransesca mentioned the long years of her spiritual devotion and service in this same letter:

> When for some 51 years, one has given in all directions to everyone and anyone – and then profundities to a certain few whom They have allowed me to give such – it is truly giving one's entire self.
>
> And then comes the fate of the 'giver' that a few 'understand' or think they do – a few listen – a few 'promise' and as long as I am in their midst – they keep with the 'teachings' and with all the enveloping love. It is not my love alone – and anyone can do most anything to me, but I will fight not only lions and tigers, but the whole menagerie if they dared so much as to demean in any manner the Masters.

One felt the great respect and love Fransesca had for the Masters. Fransesca also had challenges in the physical. She worked on the aches and pains of her body that increased in the last year and a half of her life:

> We play games – because this is truly the cosmic way – the Masters way – for like a child shall we come unto Him – and children are fabulous about 'playing games' which become very real.
>
> Have tried very hard never, never to 'talk down' to anyone as though I were at a pulpit preaching the rules and laws of life. But a 'picture story' and speaking at the same level

as the rest who are listening – is the KIND way. Then no one is offended.

Fransesca received a prayer from her Master, which was shared widely:

Grant Us the Grace

O Lord, grant us the grace
That we might be worthy to hear Thy message
And having proven ourselves worthy of hearing it
May we be alert enough to understand it.

Then Lord, having understood Thy message
May we be wise enough to interpret it
And having interpreted it
May we be gracious enough to share it.
So be it.

Fransesca lived by this prayer and was true to its message for her whole life.

In another letter to a friend dated September 24, 1979 Fransesca wrote that her husband Harry had to know jewels for each month in his work as a jeweller. Her favourites were garnet, zircon and ruby. She wore a garnet and a medallion around her neck that had been given to her by a friend. She called them her "good luck" pieces as she felt a reassurance 'that all will be well' when wearing them.

Fransesca loved the picture of Jesus known as "The Smiling Christ" depicting Him holding a lamb. She had many copies of it but gave them away. Fransesca spoke to Jesus and would ask for His advice. She thought of Him as her friend. She wanted to know Jesus and would go into her sanctum for this. Fransesca would see Jesus at different times of His life, starting when He was a little baby. He became very dear to her as a holy, sacred person. She spent ten months learning about him.

Jesus referred to the Light sixteen times. When his disciples asked Him from whence He came, Jesus replied, "Know ye me not – even now for I AM before Isiah who came."

In time of troubles, loneliness or problems, Fransesca would lay her face against His and find comfort. Fransesca also had practical suggestions for challenges one may face in daily life. When there was a problem with a nasty person, she advised to concentrate on a circle of Light on the center of the forehead:

> See oneself plugged in. Trace the circle on the forehead and ask and affirm that it brings warmth and "Light, illumination and understanding." Let the light go from oneself to the other person. Fill the room with this Light, focus it on the other person. Then go and meet the person. We can all take things if we have the backbone to handle it.

It was important for Fransesca to know and to experience both sides of the scale, in order to differentiate between what was true and what was false.

For Fransesca the sanctum (altar) was a holy place. She would go into her sanctum four to six times per day, which was more often than when she was living in Oregon and San Jose.

"What attracts others to us, either our peace or our joyfulness or our buoyancy, etc. Our home is part of our personality and people who enter into it also FEEL the personality." Fransesca used to say, "When the material house is in order, then the spiritual house is in order. Then the spiritual temple will be in harmony with it."

Fransesca believed that we heal more people by joy – a touch of our hands – a touch of love – our facial expressions, than we could possibly do with medications. An exercise of healing the body involved seeing a person within a golden orb with miniature raindrops absorbing all the negatives. This heals and strengthens the body, which has inharmonies.

Fransesca taught a powerful lesson involving cause and effects. In a letter dated December 4, 1979, she wrote:

> The Cosmic is observant how we handle our "effects" no matter what they are and how they come about in our lives. How we accredit ourselves is a new cause, which gives birth to new effects.
>
> If something comes into our life, one thing or many things, then we can be sure that somewhere along the way there had been some earlier cause – which is having an effect and we are given the beautiful opportunity of clearing up that effect to the good – so we don't have to undergo the same sort of situation again. This is our personal evolution causing us to become stronger and much more reliable and resilient individuals.
>
> For example, when we look at keeping promises, we fret and fume when people don't keep their promises to us – don't call when they said they would, talk lightly about coming over and don't really do it or mean it...Ask ourselves, do I do this too? Have I done this also? Am I following through?
>
> Then let's pretend that we see as we look into the mirror of ourselves that we read clearly that we also do this or have done this. Then one knows that in a way we are being

> affected also by our own (and others) effects and so we begin to realize that we to must 'shape up.' We can put in a new cause into motion by showing others how it is when promises are broken – by pointing out a lesson, so that we can correct their error before it becomes habitual and they create many hurts.
>
> Then the negative has been turned into a good. Sometimes people single out another because they feel insecure – that if everything is going along beautifully in their department that they will think that person is covering up because 'nothing could go beautifully' all the time. If that person or others are satisfied that things are going smoothly, then they might not be needed anymore. So that person decides to find fault and criticize... That person needs to feel important. That person is unhappy. Pray that person sees themselves as a contented person, who is happy that other people are doing well.
>
> There are hundreds of souls in the world who simply cannot say "I am sorry – you are doing fine. I hear wonderful reports about you – keep up the good work." They cannot do it, it just isn't in them...and we can't expect it of them. Though we wish they would. If we are lucky and they do say one nice thing – they become angry with themselves for having gone overboard and been kindly.

In that same letter Fransesca wrote, "We are given to bear what we are worthy to bear! Consider it an honour that there is an opportunity to correct some things – and an opportunity to be stronger each day in one's beliefs." Fransesca shared her thoughts about friendships. She had many years of experience in interpersonal relationships with people. She was also a great believer in being adaptable:

> Real friends are rare. The tried and true. Adaptability is very important to learn and then live it. No matter what the circumstances are in life, no matter how WE wish they would be different, or better, adapt to whatever is going on at the moment with the best grace one can and one will grow!
>
> There are friends who come into our life, perhaps for only 2 days, 3 years, 5 minutes, one month or for all lifetime (very rare). But when the vibration of cause and effect puts us in the same vibration, same orbit for the moment, we take up where we left off – long ago and perhaps complete what we had to offer one another or undo in 5 seconds, 10 minutes, several days or months. We might grieve, feel sad but know there is ...a reason and adapt to that reason and be grateful for it. Those moments of sharing and excitation and close union. Though we may never see that person again, those moments are wonderful. So I adapt to it, accept it and am grateful for it.
>
> Adapt to each event as it takes place in the present.... We learn to adapt and through it we also learn to judge people – to take things with a grain of salt. A real friend is a rarity...good for as to take what comes along, enjoy it while it is there. Be happy in it while it is lasting and keep our eyes and ears open and one's Self open, for feeling out and reaching out for that soul bond with another.

Fransesca was walked on and stepped on. She was taken from and was taken advantage of:

But out of it all there comes a one, or a two, who are 'worthy' and the prickly bushes drop by the wayside. I bless them – we have served our purpose and will continue to do so. There are always those rare few to whom one means a great deal, a smile, a cuddle, even though I don't do anything about their personal life. I do know that they need Mama arms and if I were to pass this way not again, they would remember little of me, but the arms, hug, love and touch. That's fine with me. That's why I came.

In order to have a friend, BE ONE. Sometimes one has to be the first one to meet people. Mingle. Make the first move.

If Fransesca had not done so, she would still be sitting in a corner waiting for something to happen. She "took the bull by the horns" and made it happen:

I create my own laughter, my own happiness when there isn't anyone around. If nothing funny is happening then thank God for the gift of imagination. I can make funny pictures. Amhadra (Master) was my wonderful teacher in that. In a very tiny thing I see something funny.

That is Mastery. That is soul satisfaction. Then one becomes proud of themselves and justifiably so.

I could rant and rave and become bitter over what some people DON'T DO. I could write a hot letter to a number of people who haven't kept word, but I have also learned to realize that THEY JUST DON'T KNOW ANY BETTER and they think nothing of it. They still have a long way to go, so I can feel pity for them, that they have this long road ahead of them and then just drop it. Why become annoyed about it? We do at first, but then we also throw it away!

Even though Fransesca was spiritually lonely, she was always loving, kind and generous. She made anyone who came to see her feel welcome and like they mattered.

Chapter Eight

Toronto

In a letter to a friend Fransesca commented on the popular expression of "soul mate:"

> We prefer spiritual mate to the word soul mate simply because soul mate has been so misused throughout the ages, while the true mating is a spiritual one – that is, two halves being total complements of one another. The soul mating is a holy relationship since the beginning of existence and always has been – the two halves of an apple – and no other halves can become the total whole. Spiritual matings are MATINGS of the two soul selves! These 'halves' know one another for through that very law of atoms (soul seed) they come together 'as one.'

Her Master told a beautiful story that was mystical and allegorical concerning "the mating." It came to be known as "The Apple Story:"

Let us pretend that you have a group together and have 24 apples. One for each person. Then let each one cut their apple in half and each one drop their halves in a large container. Mix the container a little and pass the basket around. Ask each one to choose two halves and try to put them together.

You will see that ONLY two halves will fit, yet as you find your own eventually after all 24 matched theirs, you will note that there is the core that runs through the centre of each apple. This is equivalent to the soul spark – the spark of God which lives in EACH HALF. You will also see that the seeds in the apple are equally divided, or maybe one seed was sliced that compares to the polarity to the two halves for each half is BOTH MALE AND FEMALE but one half has a plus quality. The other half a minus quality is predominant. One side is PLUS and one side is NEGATIVE and totally balanced. Thus just that PARTICULAR PAIR completes the whole. This is a Cosmic situation to begin with – the pairing or waiting of the Seed Atom which constitutes therefore the SPIRITUAL or (Cosmic) mating!

...At times they will be in the physical embodiment together. Other times, they overshadow one another (one Cosmic, one on earth). At times they come together in other relationships. Knowledge of being of the same tree is their root knowledge. There are other trees in God's garden. We are never without that "half" somewhere.

Spiritual mates do not fight or hurt one another – they are content as they are like one another. We are mated in the

Spirit – in the soul – in our essence – in our ideals – our loves – urgings – devotions.

The "apple story" was also a lesson about a spiritual tree:

It was a lesson to depict the spiritual tree. When they started to move around in class and found their half and put it with their apple and lo and behold they had the whole apple. They had the two halves that belong together. So what holds the two halves together? It is the law of polarity, the law of vibration. The two halves of the apple have the same core in the middle. The same core that runs through every apple in that tree. In order to be a whole apple, it has to have its other half...

But what is in them is that same light of being and that Light of Being goes through the left side. Move these two halves apart and each side has part of the core, each side has moisture and essence in it, but just a little different in vibration. One side is negative, one side is positive and polarity holds it together. This is natural law.

A seed is something we give birth to. The thought is the seed. It's the idea. An idea, story is a seed. Everything is a seed until it has sprouted. Everything on earth which is manifest has its source and the Light is the seed. So that Light which is in us is the source and this beam of Light, every beam of Light from the Sun has two sides. Its negative field and its positive side. Also we can say it has its dark side and its light side. It has the sun side and the moon side and as it revolves, the dark side becomes the light side and light side becomes the dark side. It is constantly in its state or condition of being or becoming something else.

And what a beam of Light from the sun may cast forth is at the end of it. At the end of it is half of each. It goes forth into manifestation. As it is upon earth and in earth and in another, it is its manifest.

It has to form a picture story in a person's mind. The cosmic seed...the soul which is a personality is a God soul. It is atomic in structure. The Universal, natural law is that it must find its opposite so that it might become one with it.

See a great big globule of raindrop as big as an apple or pear – look at it with sun shining on it and see it go kerplunk into a beautiful clear pool and alongside of it is another one going kerplunk with it. These are two drops and as they are coming down together, because they are all Light and moisture, and filled with Cosmic elements, they unite. They fall down in this pool and seem to be absorbed within this pool. We discover they are clinging together. They are separate, because one part was more positive than the other part which was more negative. Therefore, they come together as they were one.

After swimming in this River of Life in the Cosmic stream and within ourselves we are a Cosmic Stream. They are ever alive in that and in the Image out of which they have come from that Greater Light...that pencil beam of Light is in us. It is in us!

If you were to sit on a cloud you are your soul personality. Your soul personality knows itself as soul sitting on this cloud – you are of the consciousness of your atmosphere. Before you is the Image – that great, glowing wondrous Light. You see yourself – you move towards it in consciousness and you are absorbed into that Light. You are in another direction also – you are where the Light is and so you are united with that Light and then you are One.

You know yourself as she, you know yourself as he, just like those two drops that fell into that pool. That pool we can call the River of Life on earth. We can call it our seed, we can call it our manifestation, we can call it our soul seed... It is an atom of atomic structure and it is that living part of our soul life, that spark of life. Like a seed which is in us right now...But that image which is not a body, is my Beloved Masters T. She is there in the Image. And what is Love is a third point, me, the manifest, out of the two. That is what I am.

What is the love in me? It is that son, who is also of the same Light, which I am trying, because of our Image to project, here one on earth, Love. That's my Jesus babe. That's the birth of Him in me. It was a birth which was conceived atomically eons of time. ...Out of every seed, some fruit eventually happens. It becomes first a bud, then a branch, a branch of the old tree. Then it has a little bud on it, then the bud flowers, then the flowers bear fruit. Allegorically, but we have to understand it that way. This is all within ourselves.

By 1980, Fransesca had spent fifty-two years on the spiritual path. She was tested for twenty-seven and half years and had to prove her worthiness to her Masters. Service to others was gratis. Fransesca proved that she would never give up no matter how many errors or misinterpretations were made. Once she made that commitment, the "real work" began.

Only through experience and overcoming much of sadness, hurt, distrust, frustrations and misunderstandings was Fransesca allowed to try and assist others. "That is my way and shall be until my last breath."

In 1949, Fransesca was told to "trust and obey:"

> The obeying was not difficult for I had long ago given up the Fransesca 'self'....The trust part I thought would be simple, until Mr. Doubt stood up and hollered 'let me in. I want to be heard.' And then I really had to whip myself into shape again to remember, Fransesca you promised to 'trust.' So again I trusted...when things did not come out as per what I had thought I received, I finally learned to PUT IT TO ONE SIDE.
>
> Don't worry so much. This was one of your off days. You got mixed up with other thoughts. You are not passive enough right now – you're tired and try again another time, or just let it rest. Remember all the beauties. Remember those times you did hit it right on the nail...remember the strong love union and now, let it go....
>
> I cannot take myself apart constantly. I do not run the Cosmic show.

Trusting Higher Mind and the Masters became a way of life for Fransesca. She always asked to do "Thy will." When someone asked Fransesca "Why are we here?" she would reply:

> We came into life to BE – to express ourselves (the inner Master self). Most everyone thinks that they have to do something very great in the world, become a writer, scientist, a leader, teacher, etc. Have their name in lights on

> a marquee so that the world may know them and their mission.
>
> But alas it is not that way at all. That is only EGO speaking. The true Master person is one who can give – unstintingly when needed, who serves quietly usually, who is rarely known to the world, whose love is unbounded, who serves UNSTINTINGLY LOVINGLY – who continues to do His will no matter what the circumstances are. The true missionary is one who puts Self (conscious self) to one side – to DO the greater will – to WANT for others, to be a helping hand, even if it is but a smile, a loving arm, a warm embrace, a courteous gesture. Remembering friends, being a friend in need. THOSE ARE MISSIONS! Through these forms of ministrations we are DOING for our own God, that God who is a part of us. We are exemplifying the greatest part of ourselves to the world to humanity.
>
> If we are just doing it for ourselves, to become a name in lights and to become known to the world only, then this is not humility and is not our true purpose.

This life of service was Fransesca's mission and she fulfilled it beautifully. She was thorough in her giving. She gave her time, knowledge, compassion, love and experience. Kindness was the hallmark in all she did for others.

When Fransesca started on the spiritual path she prayed to be of service. The next day she was asked to help a neighbour:

> It is being constantly on the alert to who needs me? It wasn't a big thing, but it was something. Sometimes it was only a bowl of soup, or holding someone's hand while they

> cried their heart out. Sometimes it was a pat on the back when I felt that person needed arms around them.
>
> Are these small missions? Are they big missions? Are they important? I think they are VERY important. It is what we came for, if we want to answer ourselves. We came to make our own little world in which we live a better place to be. We take 'our little world' with us every place we walk and if we take a happy and loving world with us (our magnetic field, our aura) we bring that to others. Thus in effect, we are creators just as God wished us to be.
>
> Those are PURPOSES. THOSE ARE MISSIONS.

Regarding the idea that each one of us is our own creator, Fransesca wrote: "We return again and again until we have accomplished what we came for – the PERFECTION of the individual existence each time, until we needed no further return to earth."

Fransesca was careful when offering advice or suggestions. She believed in giving choices to another:

> In my training we are never permitted to tell someone what they are to do, lest we incur some of the karmic debt in event we were incorrect. We may however give three viewpoints, three suggestions so speak as to how they can handle their problem or whatever because it must be their choice, for whatever the results are to be it is theirs to decide and to experience and to learn from.

In a letter written January 2, 1980 Fransesca wrote:

> We can only interpret according to our own evolution... We all serve in our own way in different fashions. And no matter what you explain to someone else they will

> retranslate it for themselves exactly the way they want it to mean. We are not all on the same wavelength. We don't all see one colour as the same colour, nor do we all taste things in the same way, nor feel in the same way. There is always that fraction within us which is just slightly different than another person.

Fransesca often spoke of how rare it was to have close companionship with another:

> Some of us meet with souls whom we KNOW. We just know what we do and we immediately love them and we wonder about them and how we have known them before. No doubt we really have and are touching that responsive cord of memory in each of us. It is wondrous and glorious when it happens. Sometimes it is only for a brief few minutes, other times for longer periods, but always it is a thrill to have 'found one another' AGAIN!

Fransesca said that very few people are "constant and enduring" in this world. She believed that "there is always someone around the corner we are supposed to touch lives with."

It is infrequent to meet someone one can commune with. Fransesca adopted me as her spiritual daughter. She also had a close friend in another city with whom she kept up diligent correspondence with. Another student and friend was in Texas. Eventually a three way sharing began and Fransesca would share portions of her meditations. It was in this way that her legacy lived on.

Regarding her dedication Fransesca wrote:

> I have dedicated myself these 52 years and maybe proven worthy of His overshadowing and others. Part of this has

> been my MISSION – to 'find' children of the Family Tree – to teach them – some appreciated it, some have already forgotten, but I have done that which they wished me to do...

In a letter dated January 8, 1980 Fransesca commented on giving others three chances. She lived by this rule:

> Sometimes playing it aloof pays off – I've done my share of pampering and DOING, that is a lesson I learned over and over – people who say they will 'come over' and they don't – I allow them 3 chances then just ignore them entirely – just as a casual friend. I can never BELIEVE in them totally. And most of the time I have also found that if I can hold to my principle, that after a while they realize that I am no longer there to lean on, or whatever and they want to 'make up.' Even then I keep it cool until I am more certain of them. So in a subtle fashion we can also teach a lesson to others – without saying one word, just by our doing, or our NOT doing.

Fransesca believed that there was a "wave of negativity" in the world in 1980:

> The world is filled with worry – war thoughts – rape – murders – crime – bad things – you name it. It is there in the minds of someone – in papers, TV, radio, etc. Unless one is deaf and dumb and blind they can hardly escape hearing, or seeing or learning about it. So just multiply that by a billion people (or more) who read, listen – hear, think and TALK ABOUT IT – you can realize what a wave of negativity is prevalent right now. Thus, if we are in a NEGATIVE WAVE BAND OURSELVES – a mood, we tune into that

> form of negation and begin to feel worse and worse and someone who has a hidden complex or fear, or anxiety or childhood remembrance, can lay all of it to that period – and think this is what is coming to them; when it is nothing else but general world conditions being pictured out by millions of people in their own anxieties.

Fransesca's faith was strong and unshakeable. She said:

"I am of the training which says to me, IF YOU BELIEVE, you either believe ALL THE WAY, or you don't believe at all. There have never been half measures with me."

Fransesca had a favourite saying: "Nothing but good may go forth from me. Nothing but good may come unto me." She firmly believed that "Nothing but nothing can harm us from other minds, unless we want it that way and accept it – also that we ACCEPT the thought that it CAN HAPPEN!"

When certain thoughts or memories are cleared, she advised to breathe out the negative thoughts and then to see the image in the Light. The positive will absorb it and it can then be taken in as a positive thought.

Fransesca frequently spoke of not allowing the "outside inside, because the inside is greater than any outside event."

If one has doubt about something, that doubt comes from the conscious self. When there is no doubt, then the true self or Higher self is involved.

When visualizing, Fransesca taught that it was important to mentally image the plan and see those desired plans as fulfilled. One needs to have a strong and true desire.

When one truly realizes something, then the realization comes through the route of the soul. It becomes a permanent fixture in one's life:

The necessity for thinking good thoughts, for there are consequences when one does not. We treat the mental and psychic self first. All our ills are in this psychic self – when we are emotionally upset, it is the psychic body with its comparable lenses which is ill at ease and the physical body suffers thereby.

That's why I try so very hard to have good thoughts in my mind. I have my own particular thoughts to handle to keep that mind lovely and serene – but add to it the thoughts of others who have a need, those I 'worry about' – those I wish to comfort – those who ask for something and I have to find time to do the 'something or other' then you can see that my mind isn't always empty – and it is not always my own which is carousing around up there. I am trying to unravel something for someone else. Of course this is my life and service and I don't regret it...so we have to be ever watchful what parades around up there in that brain department.

Fransesca commented about tests in the following letter:

Not everything that happens of a negative nature is a TEST! People have used this thought far too much. The Cosmic does not test us purposely. We do these things by ourselves, so we can't blame the Cosmic for it, but we ARE observed as to how we handle adversities which come into our path, and if we can handle them beautifully, graciously, then THEY know that we are ready for greater enlightenment – and further training, learning to ACCEPT what we have lovingly – gratefully and humbly – is in His way. Learning to take the knocks as they come in as spiritual manner as we can is also in His way. Adapting to situations as they arise

> and working our way out of them to the best of our ability is also in His way.

Fransesca remarked, "The ways of a teacher are not always happy ways." She worked seventeen hours a day and seven days a week. There was hardly any "nothing" time in her life:

> I write but very rarely do I receive in like kind – but then it is in my nature to remember the thank you's, acknowledgments, etc. and so it should be none of my business if others can't think that way.
>
> It is true that it is wrong if we learn something and hide it within ourselves, that is no pathway of growth either for ourselves or for those whom we have come to serve and to give. But we become a bit selective about WHO and HOW and WHAT. We would not have been given these beautiful truths, the loveliness's – just for our own selfish enjoyment – they would not wish that – but, also we learn to be very alert – choice – certain as to where it goes. One can talk around a subject and present a truth.

Fransesca used discrimination and wisdom in what was being shared and with whom. She asked Cosmic permission to convey certain communion communications.

In 1980 she began writing "Humour" or "Wisdom" pages: a newsletter on a monthly basis. Twelve to fifteen sets were mailed out with a letter. Fransesca said, "Tis my service to break down some of the gloom people have."

Fransesca found it difficult in her older years when she did not have friends or contemporaries to talk or write to. By this point, many of her friends "have gone to the land of milk and honey."

> When doing good for others – remember that it is the caring end that others receive SOMETHING good which they would not have had if person x wasn't there.
>
> How do you think I felt through the long, long years to know that I (and we) have given hundreds of hours to some human beings – grown ups – who took it freely – a few used it – many forgot – BUT for that period of time when they were under our wings they THRILLED – they were love filled and I KNEW we were giving – loving – instructing, assisting! And though the years after we left and discontinued the classes via tapes from here (another 6 years of it long distance) and they turned to other things, one of my gals said "it isn't the same Mama without your presence – we try – but you kept us in line. Even the tapes are not the same without you in our midst."
>
> How many thousands upon thousands of pages have I typed throughout the years to people? Can I say it is a waste? They just take it – often without thanks – and don't use it. How can I judge what GOOD it has all done – sometime, somewhere – to some <u>one.</u>

Practical aspects for daily living were also included in Fransesca's teachings. She was down-to-earth and logical. For example, a technique for finding employment was suggested:

> Hear things that are said in an interview. See others meeting and hiring person. See receiving a letter with news that others are hiring person. Dance and be excited opening the letter. Cross fingers for 10 minutes (second and third finger) after the interview and repeat hourly.

Setting priorities was advisable. Fransesca recommended doing necessities first. For example, if there are calls to make, do all the phone calling at one time.

With respect to the present and the now, Fransesca taught the following:

> That which was past is now present tense. It is in the NOW – because it has been impressed in memory in the seed atom, with mind and consciousness...Those memories, conditions, etc. have their continuance (in manifest) as they are again – expressed (verbally).
>
> All the memories become NOW conditions, being registered in the present – manifesting again and AGAIN in some form or another. Thus they become present day fact!

An age is 21,367 years. If we cannot complete our Mastery of Self, and do that which we came for, before the cycle has ended – then we shall need to go through another complete revolutionary cycle of time: another Age! Fransesca said that the next Age would be a mystical one.

Fransesca's life attested to her strong belief in sharing:

> Loving memories of having shared – having given something of ourselves to and for others is a reward which nothing else can compete with. If we serve as God intended for us to do – then we will all become aware that we are all equal – but each of us is serving our special qualities. In order that others might share this quality with us.
>
> This is the hardest thing I believe that anyone on a dedicated path has to bear – but it is bearable when one has a few 'someones' with whom they can talk and can share.

> Then there is a release from what is inside – so it also has a place to go to and to give to…

Regardless of age, Fransesca was youthful throughout her entire life. She played games whenever she had physical pain in order to deal with it. She used picture stories to see various parts of the body, seeing the cells happy and in harmony.

Chapter Nine

Toronto

In the Heritage pages prepared on February 4, 1989 Fransesca wrote about will and its power. Her Master dictated this segment on March 20, 1965:

> We have spoken about the meek and the weak – also regarding the humble who shall inherit the kingdom – the true kingdom of God.
>
> The meek shall inherit the EARTH – and they are LOWLY... Yet, the high and mighty are not overlords, nor souls who have taken advantage of their fellow man the high and mighty ways – merely that they have taken advantage of THEMSELVES of their Divine Heritage and claimed it beyond all others – claiming it as their RIGHTFUL heritage. They have therefore gone beyond the extensions of the average individual or the indolent, slothful and indeed the placid and oftentimes insipid...who preferred the slow and quiet way at an even pace – contrary to the zealous one who would not stand back from the flow of fire with in his own entity...

Man...was so invested with mind, Consciousness and Soul that he could rise to the stars or crawl upon the land – or sit in the twilight of Life, never having fully come awake to himself.

AWAKE TO HIMSELF: The glorious dawning of a heightened consciousness. Awake to the POSSIBILITIES – and the true potential of the Christ within. Awake to the glorified one would uproot him from his lowly seat and propel him into the dignified throne of authority.

...this lowly one is NOT the Voice of Authority – therefore this one is not even a law unto himself...The low and meek one is he who listens to all other voices – basing his thoughts, ideals and ideas upon those of other men – as he has little will of his own with which to think constructively – to reason...there is difficulty in rousing him into any form of self esteem.

Without pride in Self – life is less meaningful. Without pride and idealism or a goal towards which he may grow or strive for, he remains in the same position of quiet acceptance, acquiescence, obedient to the will of others – ever serving the line of least resistance.

He is to be pitied for he has lost much of life which passes him by whilst others evolve beyond him whose king holds the reins to the Christ of their life.

Fransesca loved helping people. She had a lifetime of experience to draw from as well as from the teachings of the Masters:

> ...Just that one other person might have been filled with joy – been helped in a way that they themselves could not see. We spread the chain, in our doing – and I'm still in there pitching, sometimes feeling that it's a thankless job, except I shall not cease unless I can't use my fingers so much, then there shall be another way found.

Fransesca offered encouragement about having goals and dreams:

> We all have dreams – we can't always have them work out – but we take what comes to hand, give thanks to the Cosmic for providing for us and directing our way into certain channels – so that we might use whatever gift or talent we have IN THE PLACE WHERE WE ARE AT – and when it is right – we will also find ourselves in some other circumstances where we CAN do even if in some small measure – that which we came to do.
>
> Send your DREAM out to the Cosmic and give it to them – and let it be worked out as to your own causes and effects and what you came here to do.

A letter written on March 19, 1980 contained a loving tribute to Fransesca from a very close friend who was like a daughter: "Always you came to our rescue when we ask – never do or have you said 'no.' Always, always you have the answer, the love, the laughter, the grace, humility, pride and mostly love."

On March 18, 1980 Fransesca had a communion about Dreams. She subsequently shared this information with me and two other students. Over the years, Fransesca recorded twenty or more tapes from meditations about dreams. She reviewed her understanding from these meditations as given to her by the Masters T. and T.

Fransesca mentions 'Mabel' in this segment, a fictitious character that Fransesca wrote and spoke about to convey a lesson, instead of pointing a finger at someone:

> Define subconscious into two manners – that subconscious which is our PERSONAL subconscious in each incarnation versus the UNIVERSAL SUBCONSCIOUS which contains the Akashic records. (past life).
>
> When someone in transition – seeing her former life from the emotional self – in picture form wakes up and earth is now an illusion. Her mental awakening begins and she becomes awake to the knowledge that she had been WITHIN the thought world of her own 'formings.' (THOUGHTS ARE THINGS!)
>
> All those thoughts 'forms' would appear to be very real and at the point of recognizing some of them as her own, it would be like looking into a mirror of herself (reflection) discovering flaws, conquered or not and seeing the subconscious 'pictures' (or forms). Passes through stage 1 (psychic, emotional effects).
>
> Stage 2 is the mental stage. More dispassionate as it recognizes what it has formed during its evolutionary path on a mental level. This entity would be like the High Self – mind...Become conscious of itself and recognizes its spiritual self.
>
> Stage 3 – Coming awake to its spiritual self and the 'formings' it had conceived while on earth. It becomes THAT – a Spiritual Being – a spiritual soul. The 3 dimensional aspect has by then lost its hold on earth, it is now more closely associated with Cosmic existence.

If this entity had 'formed' spiritual states, conditions, ideals, beliefs, goals in mortal existence, the experience in these first 3 earlier stages would be brief – and she would find herself a Spiritual Being – for thus had she 'formed' her world prior to the cosmic rebirth cycle. She would therefore be that FORM – suited to her evolutionary pattern and continue this relationship in herself and cosmic growth into the Master 'form,' Christ form etc. These are all the higher realms of her 'formings' while on earth and her REALITIES. In order for them to BE these realities – in her mortal existence Mabel would have had to know through consciousness and realization the existence of her 'formings.'

Her 'formings' would have had to be part of her daily life while on earth – with a purpose also, otherwise how could she create?...The ONLY path upward in the spiral of present life and future life is one WE HAVE PERSONALLY 'formed.' We are nothing else but what we have formed in all of our life – we have imprinted indelibly in cosmic records that we ARE – not what we like to think we are going to be 'some day' but what we are as of this moment – is what we have imprinted!

We write the copy and the copier already has the imprint. – It also has the imprinting of all our 'formings' – we can blame none other if the imprintings are not pleasant... unless we have 'reformed' them and made them whole once again!

Higher stage – existing within the planes of Being – (spiritual master, Christ formings) would be knowable to this entity – if her own 'formings' are of such nature also. She would respond through the route of her own stored memories in the Akashic record. In the Master (form) she would 'see' the mundane existence as a Dream which she had experienced now being awake to herself as SOUL. Again, the reverse order of existence so to speak.

In a following incarnation to earth life the 'memories' of the REAL WORLD (Cosmic) and all the learnings – Mabel's period of that world existence would become a part of the DIVINE REFLECTIONS IN her – which would be brought out through part 1 'dream lessons' i.e. subconscious, subjective, etc. And again she would return these dreams according to their present era consciousness, in her own way – some bringing back memories as she again grew in stature and spiritual understanding.

In the return to physical embodiment and soul stirrings lead one to certain tasks – grading one so to speak for fulfillment, conquering tendencies, desires, longing, creating greater awareness, etc. These yearnings for 'souls' Mabel had encountered in the REAL world – again in a manner becoming alive to her – as memories – would become a challenge to her to become finer, greater, and more loving as that SELF which she knows herself to fully be – for all that which was REFLECTED in her mind, would be REALITIES, to her instead of illusions.

The entity therefore would have illuminations, experiences, beyond the subconscious 'dream' state.

The Realities of Light – Soul – Love – Beings – all as FORMS would be part of her soul memory – out of the

> Akashic records, primordial substance, far beyond the personal subconscious of which she had formerly been so conscious. Within her True Self (soul self) all would be existent – through the route of Universal subconscious, the true Akasha.
>
> All is Divine Reflection – if the Light of Being so burns within her that it lightens and brightens her path, she is THAT – which she had 'formed' in her previous span of Time (or times) having recognized and known herself – and others – for their True Selves – with or without the flaws which humankind would see.
>
> She would thus recognize those whom she encountered in life because of those 'formings' – they had likewise been creating, and these 'formings' were much like her own – or familiar to her, NOT in body sense – WITH body – but in a SOUL sensing, through formings and evolution of that personality.
>
> The Divine Reflections are like unto a mirror – naught is observed or hidden from the Realm OF THE REAL WORLD – or Divine Mind.
>
> Therefore, in mortal existence again, the call of the Soul is loud and clear for That One – who would hear it and desire to do its bidding, this is Soul's Yearning to BE Wholly Divine!

In a letter dated April 23, 1980, Fransesca wrote about her sense of pride. There is a contrast to the writing when her Master dictated from when Fransesca wrote:

> Like everyone else I do have low days, days I just want to crawl under the house and hide, or not talk. I always prefer

> to do my own solving with myself BY MYSELF – and to fight out certain conditions, frustrations, or whatever it may be – and I MUST do it alone. I am not a leaner, though sometimes it would be nice to just flop – and lean. Guess the Cosmic had a strict tug on me – I must not fail them. So at those times I am not fit for humanity until I get ME straightened out.

Fransesca was a great believer in letting go of her frustrations. She wrote:

> Don't let frustration be beyond the normal bounds of frustration. It is good to get it out of our system – we have to have a place to PUT IT – but then when it is out – IT'S OUT! Get frustration one has out from within even if it doesn't go anywhere.

Fransesca also said that "One has to be one's own strength. Everything has its own space and time. Every situation needs to resolve itself."

Fransesca was a master at working on herself. Even though she had undergone rigorous training years before in clearing herself, she kept at it. Fransesca advised one of her students that:

> We do not all have the personality to make everyone like us – most of the time – and we don't always know what sort of circumstances they have at home, at work, with other people – either – so we try to make allowances. Some people can handle the changeability – moods of others – some can't and most often it is cuz we can't handle our own changeabilities – our own moods – our own variables.

Fransesca was a life-long learner and believed that experiences were the best teachers. "So in everything we do, try to do, etc., we learn something." When there were no responses to the "Humour Pages" newsletter she commented:

> I often wonder what is wrong with the human race who are so reluctant to comment about things? And then I think, 'they're not with it yet – they're growing too – someday they'll get there!" That is true of course, but it doesn't make it simple for me – though I too am trying NOT TO NOTICE IT."

In a letter to a student dated March 19, 1980, Fransesca wrote about teaching through the route of pictures in her classes in San Jose. She created pictures on large sheets of paper and taped them to the wall. Then the lesson became more understandable:

> Pictures are the Cosmic language – they precede the idea, then the thought, which is finally 'pictured' out through the route of consciousness – then spoken – then BECOMES A MANIFESTATION on the physical level of the former Cosmic idea which is precipitated. So few people understand how powerful this can be, until sometimes I tell them to ask themselves how they feel when they go to a movie – A good movie, that is. Do they feel themselves part of the script – the movie or do they project themselves into one of the actors, actresses, townsfolk or whatever? Are they living it along with them – and do they come home with some picture idea in their mind, still feeling the impact of that 'good' movie? If so, they can realize how some individual who is trying to get some message across is really giving them a movie – providing they have the personality

> and deep inner feeling themselves TO GET IT ACROSS. In other words to be a good actress, actor – portrayer of the 'message.'

Fransesca continued instructing using pictures when speaking to people. The teachings came from her Higher Self: "When we have a need, send out a Cosmic petition that one has this need and ask to be directed towards it or have it come TOWARDS you. Then release it and let it go."

Fransesca could be any age to suit a condition, for her Master Self was ageless. My close relationship to her as a spiritual daughter involved a fifty-year difference in age. She often spoke of "the natural way being the Master's way." We had a loving rapport that was natural and there was no difference felt in our ages. Very few people have a chance to talk, to laugh, to love, to be silly and to be deep. To be considerate of each other and feel good just being together. It is God-given when it happens.

Fransesca believed that the world conditions were difficult. On this matter she said:

> This age we're in is in a sad state for many reasons. Drugs #1 – too much laxity #2 – no one coming through – #3 – a total lack of discipline – simply because – who cares? When children feel this (so sad) they also feel, "well if they don't care, why should I bother?" Also they feel "they don't own me – what did they give me anyway? – we have discontent and unhappy kids and parents too. Wise parents – will love and let go – and let live! They will counsel – advise and love and let go! If they've done this well in formative years – the children will try to show them how responsible they can be – it is then a matter of pride. Pride in themselves first and wishing that someone else be proud of them also. We

all need someone to be proud of us – that helps us to do even greater things.

When one encounters a heaviness or darkness in either one's surroundings or somewhere else:

> ...it helps to use the "Flood Light" on the forehead – before we leave the house. Then pretend there is a 300-watt bulb in it – stop over near a light socket and pretend to plug it in. Go all lit up – shining a pathway ahead of oneself, preparing the way. Believe in the Light which is there – see coming or going to each one in that negative atmosphere and bringing light to the dark places!

This was a technique that one could use in any situation that required more Light. Fransesca taught that we are Master/Mistress of our own situation. If we are unable to 'Master' "our self (the small self), then how can we hope to ever <u>be</u> Master – as an example to ourselves?"

On April 26, 1980, Fransesca shared a portion of her meditation recorded on August 17, 1964:

> The Eye of the Soul which sees and knows all...Can you not compare the growth of all in nature to the same growth in your fellow man – each on the plane of their own being – or nature? It is then the 'seeing' which mortal speaks of – or is this the invisible thread the Invisible World in which the Light is the knowledge – the Truth of Being? Are you not therefore that the 'seen' is not always the 'seen' for the Infinite is the Unseen – which must become realized before it can be seen. Sight is in many fashions – and not the fashion alone at sense – but the Nature of Realization.

As part of a three way sharing with her students on May 11, 1980, Fransesca wrote:

> ...when we are working with other people who have a need – there is NO problem whatsoever in SEEING all those beautiful potentials which are part of that individual's particular personality and what they are REALLY able to accomplish. I also have no difficulty in seeing them as whole – well-strong-at point of contentment, etc. etc. but to SEE all of this for myself is another thing...
>
> I must SEE everything. It has been my training – so how could I SEE Master T. as a form...We all need a 'something' some kind of approach to make things real to ourselves. Words are NOTHING – unless they CONVEY something to our mind – some picturing, etc.
>
> I need someone to listen to me also – and to help me over my own stupidity – and straining to be JUST RIGHT in THEIR eyes.

Fransesca described how many people are born with a need. Hers was never money or prestige:

> I've always yearned for love – to be loved and to be Beloved! And, due to my inferiority complex, I had a huge battle to respect and honour my Self. I think if I have any real need, it is for respect from others and for love. Not applause, etc. cuz that's merely ego and usually when it comes from others – it doesn't always come from the heart.
>
> In a way it's why I've filled much of that empty space with pets. I was without a dog (or bird) only 6 months in my entire life – and when I moved to Toronto, it was nearly

> 3 years before I had Tutu (parrot) though I wanted my cockatiels.
>
> We all need people to talk to – write to – commune with, etc. and if we don't have the right one (or ones) to hold in that 'space' of love, it is empty. That's when the rhythm is (jagged) etc. as we try to fill the blank spaces with material doings to establish some kind of Order again. But is not the same for "IT" can't hug or laugh or smile, or talk – it is but a substitute.

Fransesca nurtured her relationships with people. She was respected and loved by many. In a letter dated June 13, 1980, Fransesca noticed that people were not as careful about acknowledging the receipt of a letter or card as they once were. The importance of doing so changed with an increase in 'taking' rather than in 'giving.' She believed that:

"If people don't learn it this time, next lifetime will come the lesson, they will sit and wait and wait and wait for what they are expecting and it won't be forthcoming."

Fransesca's Master taught that one of the first requisites in Mastery – and 'becoming' Masters was courtesy – promptness – keeping word – and 'returning the borrowed.' Fransesca lived by these requisites. She was a Master soul in her doings for others.

On June 29, 1980, Fransesca wrote about being neglectful:

> Whenever we personally recognize that in some manner we have been lax, faulty – perhaps neglectful of our own 'doings' or (non-doings) and we have seen for ourselves – THEN we are making a huge step forward.

> The secret is to try not to repeat the performances! As the little ones are out of the way and we learn to realize 'they weren't so bad after all.' Then start on larger flaws.
>
> Take just one – think about it, analyze it – be honest with oneself and promise that next one we will whip.
>
> Don't put negatives back inside – build some pretty pictures. Put pictures of how wonderful it felt when one did what one said they would. The little child in us loves games – make it a game – but they are no fun if there isn't some new and or some NOTICE that we have accomplished something.

Fransesca was a highly disciplined individual. Her meditations, communion periods, correspondence and the preparation of meals were all examples of excellent time management skills. "Discipline must have some token reward to it – because one wants approval from one's own higher self, the Master Self. One feels much happier then."

Fransesca believed in using time wisely. "I cannot waste moments." She discussed habits by stating:

> ...We 'form' them just like we form all other type of thoughts. We can 'reform' a new way of accomplishing something so that we have left over 'time' for something which is very important.
>
> I do have faults but I do have one thing which I can claim – and it is that I TRY. I don't like 'me' when I fail – when I can't handle things, when I seem to be overcome with annoyances, frustrations, etc. I don't like ME either when my body acts up – and think why in heck does this have to

happen just now? It is not a punishment – but it is merely a fact of nature – and I must learn to handle Mother nature (ha ha) much more nicely and not become rattled. Of course I could also give myself a lot of excuses (which people do) and tell ME that I have a right to be annoyed, etc. but then I also answer ME and say, 'BUT DO I?' Each soul must work out their own salvation – I can only offer a shoulder or help IF I AM ASKED (and not before) – meanwhile I better learn to tend to my own garden and keep those weeds out, right?

Chapter Ten

Toronto

In a letter written on June 11, 1980, Fransesca mentioned that she typed 1,149 pages since January of that year. She kept up her correspondence and teachings into the last few years of her life. She wrote that what was being reflected back to her from another's personality – the real soul personality her Master self can see. The conscious self might not be as aware of it unless in very high consciousness.

She explained that each Master has their own form. Fransesca drew portraits of some of the Masters in pastel when she was living in San Jose. These were inspired images of what she saw. Fransesca had some assistance with the drawings as she had not had any previous experience. On June 19, 1980 Fransesca wrote a response to a student who asked about 'form.' She explained that:

> We are always forming something – we 'form' in our minds, an idea perhaps of what a Christlike being in OURSELVES might be. How would you explain to someone else what someone with Christ-consciousness is like? We have come

to that place in our evolution where we have some vague or perhaps deeper realization at what a Christlike being – Christlike consciousness might be. If we do not have it within ourselves as yet – we have not formed it. We are also that part of forming! And if our FORMINGS have been good – then we KNOW them for they are within us and we are like THAT! We have in truth given birth, we have conceived, we have BECOME that which we COULD conceive!!

How could we explain to another what the 'form' of love is? HOW? It is not a material thing, only – it is a development out of one's self, the true inner soul nature which comes forth in a FORM of our realizations. Can you explain to others that LOVE is a shape – that love is an energy – that love is a BODY primarily on a physical level? Can you 'form' this as an ideation? An abstract condition? – or is it comparable to an essence – a perfume – a radiation – a 'something' which others might feel? Then how does one equate it in order that others might relate to it and say "Ah, now I understand I know what love is – Nay – it is not the word formings – it is birth formings within the SELF!

Love becometh a RADIATION – a TANGIBLE tho seemingly ethereal or evanescent quality and the QUALITY of one's soul and its personality is ETERNAL. All formings are ETERNAL! They are formed in the year 1900, they are reformed to greater extent, in the year 1950 – they have grown and developed in vaster and more expansive form, by the year 1980 – and they are YOU. YOU – the entity in mortal realm, are the 'former' one who has created, one who has made of itself, a FORM from many conceivements – and growth patterns.

> Man creates the 'form' of a mental self, his own evaluation of what a MIND BEING might be – to its highest aspects – and it becomes his FORMINGS. HE HAS DONE SO, HE himself or herself has created such...Each trembling effort, each moment in time, when the soul growth progresses, that 'forming' becomes greater, more wondrous, more powerful, until indeed the Entity becomes the MASTER self in body pattern, body shape – reflecting all the glories of the universe from within itself. It is then walking amongst men, walking WITH the body – to the far corners of the earth. As the true Master – the Master formings throughout its existences having finally come to the point of resolution, that it is FORMED now – within a body – within a soul – vehicle as One who has accomplished, who hath overcome, who hath seen in its own FORM being complete...It be not a concrete thing, such as man knoweth this substance – but the intangible – growing pattern which formeth ITSELF – thorough knowledge, endeavours, yearnings, cravings. – strugglings, always to greater and more noble heights – until it becomes the GREATEST, the finest, the wondrous FORM of its birthings! (Master T.)

When the Master dictated and Fransesca was the channel, the writing was distinct and different from when Fransesca – conscious self, wrote. Oftentimes letters were interspersed with the writing of her Master. "I will fight tooth and nail that NO ONE insults the Masters who have given all of us so much. There is nothing we write, which I write alone."

Fransesca kept a meditation book over the years in which she transcribed the recorded meditations. They consisted of notes taken from tapes channeled for Master T.

On July 5, 1980, Fransesca commented that:

> The broken word is from the mouth of man, but the KEPT WORD is God's word. Coming through the mouth of man for God does not break His word. We can 'hear' when it is man's word and also can HEAR when it is God's word.

It was a good idea to:

> ...Take lovely thoughts at bedtime – read something pleasant – it is peace producing...I figure out ways and means to get me out of myself. I have not perfected by any means the high, high uppers all the time, but these past 3 years have been the most consistent negative in so far as health is concerned, and I sometimes rebel at it, like a spoiled child. I want to stamp my feet and say 'it's not fair, it's not fair' etc. but of course I know whatever it is – is because of some NATURAL law, not a punishment. I don't carry guilt on that score thank heavens, the only guilt that I have ever worked years ago – but then at THAT time I thought I had a lot of energy and health 'left over' to use. As we become older we realize that it would have been much wiser to have saved some of it for that proverbial rainy day.

Fransesca also tried very hard to keep things impersonal when speaking to or writing others.

> Love is the impressing agent – Love is powerful energy. Love has many forms. Love impresses itself in form – for Love is a form of it's consciousness, which is in levels,

> degrees of energy. We can form it in physical, spiritual, personal and impersonal manner and in Universal manner.
>
> Others FEEL the radiations of love energy, which impresses the 'picture stories' indelibly in memory.

People left Fransesca's home uplifted ninety-nine percent of the time. "The Love lives on as the pictured messages and lessons are carried as a MEMORY, as a radiation, emanation and Cosmic energy, all of which is healing." Fransesca commented on building the Christ within:

> Obedience and patience are necessary. Personal Master takes over. In the communions, all is mind to mind. Beyond this is heart knowing and sensing.
>
> Seeing, knowing, sensing, feeling is as one sense, the sixth sense. It is also the plane of Light or the Soul Light of God. It is not through mortal objective or through the subconscious. Not through the astral realm, but through the Cosmic realm. The Soul Light pierces darkness and shadow.
>
> Light is mind and is in the breath. This is electrical. Water is necessary for building the form in us. Do not fill the form without water. One is building the Christ form. Christ is built with the word. The mortal plane does not build. Christ in man is the creator and His mind and breath are the fixators of the Image.

In a letter to a friend written on March 16, 1975 Fransesca wrote that no one receives one hundred percent of the time in meditation:

> Sometimes we don't interpret properly. Human quality gets in the way. Very often our personal feelings, thoughts we are holding are mixed up in our reception. If we are 75% correct in our reception and interpretation we are considered to be most exceptional.
>
> Giving examples are the finest story lessons because they are not abstract or something which is only nice to say – but from one who has lived through the 'story' and can tell about it – it is an EXAMPLE worth quoting or talking about.

When Fransesca knew she had to move from Oregon, she wondered what she could do to earn a living. What could she undertake at her age? (60?) She received, "You will be provided for." At that time she was interested in sleep talk tapes. Fransesca was told her voice soothed people. She made some tapes for friends. Fransesca asked in meditation whether or not she would be doing tapes and received a positive affirmative reply. She assumed it would be sleep tapes.

However, it was not making sleep tapes in San Jose. It was transcribing Master tapes for various class members that helped pay for rent, food and many of her expenses. Sometimes Fransesca transcribed up to 30 tapes per week. There were two lectures per tape which she sold for $5.00 each.

This is an example of how one word "tapes" which was affirmed, had an extremely different meaning from that which her conscious mind believed:

> Sometimes the Beloved of our heart relays a message that is lost or mixed up. When the Beloved is needed on a spiritual mission the soul to soul route is instantaneous situation – it is KNOWING before the thought is spoken, etc.

This is the union Fransesca had with her Masters. Fransesca became God's spokesperson.

When one asks a question in meditation and there is doubt or one isn't quite sure, STOP! Change the subject – get away from it...Because when we are in a state of DOUBT, we are in a negative condition and we could not be certain of ourselves.

We can give thanks and promise to return to it the next day, or an alternative would be to leave the room and verbally ask and then wait to hear if we feel a 'nothing' feeling or a 'blah' feeling – then one isn't on the right track...but if the whole being from the INSIDE out was thrilled and genuinely happy and felt GOOD...then one knows it was good. YOU CANNOT FEEL A DEEP INNER SPIRITUAL GLOW unless one is IN TUNE WITH...the subject, thought, thing, condition or personality!

Wanting the truth is important. Wanting accuracy is wanting assurance of it being correct...

Still, the greatest truth and PROOF of knowing is from the INSIDE to the outside. Be in the quiet ...stand still... there will be moments of doubt... and then joyous days... moments when there appears to be an absolute ONENESS even if for a split second with COSMIC UNION and COSMIC LOVE were worth it, one thousand times over.

Such is the case in times of difficulty.

It has proven to me once again, that even though one might be in great distress mentally and though we cannot sleep and are disturbed if we are really trying – and truly

> desirous of being as spiritual as possible about mundane things – that we CAN and DO receive assistance. It also proved that one CAN surmount the very crude language, the hurt barriers – inner turmoils and distresses and rise into higher consciousness.

Fransesca was a great believer in sharing and did so lovingly and generously.

"For there are always my reasons for sharing, in order that another person might feel something which they hadn't felt before, and thereby have some joy, even if maybe second handed joy."

Fransesca spoke of the power of the spoken word. She endorsed speaking verbally in one's communions and meditations. Sound therefore became so important to Fransesca versus that of a silent mediation. Her Masters without words would be boundless and unmanifested. As Fransesca was a channel for the Masters through the spoken word, in a silent meditation, They would not manifest. The spoken word was necessary for the manifestation of Their thought. Her mind is heard and her love is felt. The Master manifests through her.

Fransesca made a distinction between feeling and emotion. Her consciousness is feeling in the communion periods. There is a response from the Masters to Fransesca's questions and ideas that were discussed during these periods. She knows that the Masters exist in her imagination. "This I know because I feel the blending of consciousness and His mind – and my consciousness feels and accepts this as a reality."

In a letter written March 14, 1977, Fransesca described that the Master presence and the Master vibration are signified by seeing gold in her aura. The electromagnetic field is the aura.

On March 16, 1977, Fransesca wrote about Green Hill in Oregon. She had loving memories of living on the Oregon hilltop. Her conscious self felt this and felt her love:

> To be led to a place is not often as important to the physical entity as it is important to the Soul Self, for it is through this route of Oneness with THE Self, that the conscious entity can come into its own true nature – communing with itself...The impact is SPIRITUAL! Which would naturally affect the physical wellbeing.

Fransesca believed that the Earth was a schoolroom in which one could grow, learn and evolve:

> As long as we are a physical vehicle we will have situations to solve to conquer, to learn to overcome, decisions to make, things to alter, etc. Earth is our schoolroom – for earth experiences – thus it isn't always easy, cuz the environment into which we are placed is not always conducive to the best of what we want. But we can't always have what WE want (conscious self) otherwise there would be no overcoming, no growth – if everything were just our way. And lots of humans sure would be in one heck of a mess wouldn't they if they had it THEIR way? Witness all the sadness of the kids of this recent era – doing their 'own thing' the way they want it – and can one say that there is any spiritual growth for them or even any mental or physical growth? Nay – such sad things they are. So, those of us who have chosen a way to trod, – find ourselves beset with more things – simply BECAUSE we are on a way – a Path and thus we are always being faced with some decisions, such as is it MY WAY – or is it the Cosmic way? God's way

> – Master's way...but of course I want to do what the Cosmic loves wish me to do – if THEY wish it and approve – of course I will obey, no question whatsoever about it....I just wouldn't know how to stick to MY personal preference, or personal ideas. Most of the time of course I come to the conclusion that I really didn't have any personal idea at all, "they" place the ideas there and see to it that I bring them out so that WE can discuss them later...is wonderful.

During a visit to Fransesca's home, she suggested a visualization to me to help facilitate that the Higher Self leads. It consisted of:

> Imagine a car (vehicle) – open the back door, slump down in the seat as though you were stretching your legs way out and half close your eyes. Then picture in your mind that in the front seat, holding a wheel is a lovely shimmering FORM – with some manner of 'shape' – which has eyes in its head, fingers, toes and all over its body (so the Cosmic love)... and that IT knows you are there – but that you are being a nice girl and not interfering with the Driver of the vehicle, for after all, she has already passed all her driver's tests. Now she is ready to move. The vehicle moves quietly and effortlessly...and you are merely sailing on soft clouds... she just slides along serenely and HARMONIOUSLY and you are ENJOYING the ride... she LEADS and you only have to ENJOY and be at peace. The HIGHER SELF knows the way...when you step into the back door and relax, start talking to HER – talk about a problem and that you aren't certain what tactic to take, for the right road to use to get to where you want HER to take you, or where the Father wishes you to go, or to do...you are WILLING to follow and

> give thanks that it is so. State the problem and say something like "I have now turned it over to YOU – and I won't interrupt or think about it anymore. I'll follow YOUR lead when we get there cuz you are the Driver and I'm your student and I'll learn from you' and then LET IT GO.

Fransesca made mention of the term "channel" as it was a popular term. She made a distinction that:

> Channel is used so commonly nowadays, everyone wants to be a channel or says they are, etc...so many feel that it is like another body lives within our body, another PERSON and that that person (entity) is talking through us, etc. It makes it feel rather 'common' for me, anyway. The captain of my soul is SHE who leads it and HE is ONE with HER as she is leading it or vice versa. The vehicle is merely obedient and becomes LIKE that one who leads. It is not a 'taking over' of the body, mind, etc. like those who think who speak of channeling, although the term is good, it does not quite represent the beautiful cosmic relationship. (anyway to me it doesn't).

Fransesca believed there were two kinds of people in this world. Namely, head people and heart people. Heart people can understand head people, but head people cannot understand heart people.

Fransesca felt a oneness and a sense of universality with others. She had a "Mama" heart. As an Aquarian, the world was her home and everyone a brother, or child, or sister. Fransesca was grateful for every moment spent with her Masters. For her, the greatest disgrace is that she would bring shame or dishonour to the Cosmic souls she loves.

Chapter Eleven

Toronto

On August 12, 1980, Fransesca had to have surgery, as cancer had been found in one of her kidneys. She spent three to four weeks in the hospital. Even with a health condition, she prepared a newsletter to give people something to make them laugh, smile or share with others:

> I have kept up my mood quite well...except for some of the long night hours. But for the most part I try not to think what is ahead – and find ways and means of touching hearts with other people for whom their load is of course the biggest load in the world. Sometimes I feel I had to be in here just at this time for a purpose – so I accept that purpose for service and loving has been my whole life.

In keeping with her habit for expressing gratitude, Fransesca wrote a general letter of thankfulness after returning home from the hospital on August 25, 1980. She received 99 cards, 68 letters, 11 bouquets, 18 house garden plants, 19 long distance calls and 47 home calls:

> Each of you have brought a special love-joy to me during my most trying and critical moments of my life. Thank you for your love and friendship – your prayers – for without it all I am certain my condition would be more difficult. God bless.
>
> First and foremost I love you. Without all of you and your support things would have been quite bleak but I had my fighting clothes on and am determined that inasmuch as I was born a Meyer person – that THAT strain in my makeup can overcome many things – it has done so before and there is no reason on earth why it can't do so again!

Fransesca loved Mahalia Jackson and her music. Mario Lanza and Jussi Boerling were others who provided a boost when she needed one. Scheherazade by Rimsky Korsakov was another favourite of hers. Fransesca said, "Music of a certain type is my lifesaver."

A communion period discussing 'Image' was held on November 18, 1980. It was shared with Fransesca's students:

> There are levels and planes of image forming. Form of feeling, the Master form, the Christ form and the God form.
>
> We don't always 'get' something because we are not always ready.
>
> Meaning of image is not the average person's definition. Pictures that we make, as we see something or hear a lesson, or are talking or are listening to something, are being created in the mind and become part of the subconscious.

We react to a beautiful scene. That which we see, this causes a picture to rise in our minds. Pictures are three-dimensional and they're created by us, our thoughts, conversation, listening, what we respond to, through the five senses and become part of the psychic self.

Faith is good and has to produce something, which causes belief. Belief causes knowing. All three of the 3D world. Faith to belief to knowing. First three steps. Emotion and five senses still involved in this particular process of faith to belief to knowing. Understand from a knowing and intellectual level and we say I know, but are not yet feeling it from the 4D world (which is world of feeling). Feeling then we are in the so called "as above, so below" and we feel through the route of heart and soul. The physical senses are not part of this.

What, where and how is that Image? After we feel something, we have to realize it. There must be a realization of what we are feeling, because then there is an illumination. It is beyond the point of saying "I know." Illumination. Realization is a psychic sensation in this consciousness. It is a sensation that the soul transfers to our mind, through our consciousness and then we can say, "I've realized that, I've had an illumination." Nothing to do with the five senses. Then there is an excitation and we are thrilled. Illumination. Luminous light. One is illumined, one is Light. We are in the Light. What we are in the Light. What are we? I am that Light. I am THAT I am. What is my THAT I am? I am a reflection of THAT which I am. What is THAT which I am? That is the Image.

That is the Light out of which the Light, the Image, out of which I am, mortal self, the reflection! ...Image is total Light. Image is total truth. We are a reflection of the Image which is total Light and total truth and pure. It is not a false Image. It is God source, God essence, God Light, from when we have come. There is no darkness there. There is no opposite to its Light!

Only man makes false and distorted images. Man makes a false God in himself. Man, in himself as he looks upon his body and finds fault in it – these are distortions. The pure image casts no distortions, no distorted reflections...

I am Light. I am a reflection of that greater Light. The Image desires to be in us.

Let this body be filled with Light...The Image is pure and bright. Jesus spoke this. "I am the Light" Jesus said. "Come unto me." He was saying to his disciples that they should come unto the Light and there would be no darkness for them. He was the Image of God. He was asking his disciples to come to Him. But they saw Him as a mortal walking amongst men. His reflection was luminous. His was the healing Light. He began to manifest this so powerfully. "BY my Light shall ye know me. Make thy way Light." Walk the pathway of Light. How many phrases like that have been laid right in our lap and we didn't see it!

Now I think the cure, if you want to use this word, is having a total realization to the best of our abilities, that the Light is and that we are a reflection of it, reflections out of it, that it likewise exists in us...Radiate through our psychic self and remove the darkness. Darkness that we have perhaps

> put there unknowingly, unwittingly and hoping for it to be eradicated. Now they can be eradicated through our reality and the realization of this greater light.

'Image' Part 2 was discussed during a communion period on January 15, 1981. It concerned the subject of Light and how to use it. Also discussed was the process of clearing. Both were included in a letter to a student:

> BE-ing is Light. That which is the Image as explained earlier, is our soul self, our pure soul self is that true Image out of which we have come. And inasmuch we have come out of it, we are the Light out of that soul Image. In other words, Fransesca's Higher Self is the soul image of Fransesca, because this is the BE-ing reflection on earth. Master T. is a part of that Master BE-ing so that the male and female aspect is the reflection in, Fransesca the mortal, but in me as soul and its reflection the Image is not a form out there in space. The Image is a glowing, glorious, wonderful, fantastic, magnificent of glowing Light. It is like a miniature Sun out of which we have come.
>
> We are one of the strands out of the Source. We are one of the beams out of the Source. We are one of the Lights out of the Source, and that Source is brilliant, dazzling, energetic, glowing, stimulating God-given Light. That is the Image of these strands which came unto us and are part of our body and are reflections out of that Light.
>
> If we were to make a mortal picture, like if we were to put our finger up into the air and there is this lovely Sun that has that has all kinds of rays A, B, C, D, E, etc. Of F, that's my ray. That is my beam of Light in me! That picture to help

comprehend that great, wondrous, situation and condition of BE-ing, okay. But that's making a picture, but it gives us a something that we can compare by. But it is <u>not</u> a form of someone because when we do this, we have subtracted ourselves from that God Source out of which all of us have come.

We are all Suns and parts out of that God given Sun Light. And therefore I feel, I feel for others, because they also move through me and are a part of me, because they are of the same source. You are a part of me, and I am a part of you. Because when you're not feeling well and I'm not feeling well and when I don't hear from you, something isn't right I don't always know what. But in me something says and speaks to that ray and beam of BE-ing of which we are a part says to me, someone needs you, so and so is happy, down, joyful. This is not clairsentience. This is that soul thread that is in me and begins to vibrate from that ray and my BE-ing which I am and touched by so many, begins to exert itself. These are mortal words – exert...and I know at once and then I mortal self exerts myself to see what I can do to help.

When we love, we love so exquisitely, another someone, because they have touched our soul chord of BE-ing. We are vibrating then on a God plane, we are vibrating then on a much higher source and that is God in us....

Suddenly came the realization that it is all in me, as reflection, that Light. That reflection, that Light and that golden, glowing Sun, God-Source ----I am a reflection of it!!!!! I am my soul personality. I AM. I am THAT I am. And THAT is the ancient name of God and what we have conceived of THAT to be, that is what God is to us. And what I AM – my true soul, my total identity, my total personality, is what I have conceived in all life cycles. Until I am like THAT that perfect forming, perfect realization, I will still be mortal, trying to reach for it. When we have come to realize that God-hood and God-Self in us, then we are beyond being a reflection. Then we have become that Image. We have become that true Light, which sheds Light upon the earth. It sheds God's Light to others, for it is its own Light, its own pure Light.

It is no longer distorted, nor a distorted reflection (just like looking into a pool, and throwing a rock in the pool and suddenly all the lovely little things that we saw in the pool that were clear before. Our face is distorted. We have muddied it (the pool, that clear pool of mind). We have muddied it by distortions of ill beliefs, frights, fears, anxiety, negation, panics, the words of mortals, the words of other people, who have filtered through our consciousness, who have filled our subconscious with stuff. We have accepted that and believed them to be true, so our clear pool of mind is muddled. And mind, being part of the body, causes body to be confused, muddled and unhappy and miserable and hurts. We do not cure that overnight by some great adjustment, or by taking certain types of pills that by night make it all well.

There is a process of learning and evolving but then we grow. Each time we grow, that pool becomes clearer. Now how can we use these thoughts and apply them?..I do not tell other people what to do, unless I do it myself and prove it out. You know that from my years of talking and doing. Not just for a few months. Our work is deep and serious and profound and meaningful and I must prove this to myself day after day to the Cosmic or I am not worthy. And I do not wish to disgrace them for the investment they have put in me.

...This is how I was taught and what to do:

When there is a hurting area in the body, or hurting thought, or fear, or frustration, anxiety or panic thought, it is negative, isn't it? It comes from the subconscious. How do I get rid of it? And suddenly this lovely thing transpired. Around us, in our magnetic field are many thoughts and thought pictures. You know that. Master T's balloon story. The balloon has to be filled with something beautiful. Everyone understands the balloon story. But when one has a deep hurt, it's terribly hard to put something beautiful there.

As we take a shallow breath, we are to breathe in (law that positive absorbs the negative). IF there are thoughts out there that we don't want, we have to take out what's inside and put it outside. There are people who come here and they feel better, because they have put outside all their negatives to me, and then I have to get rid of them.

Let me pretend, that inside of me, in my body, in my subconscious, is a few thoughts that I don't want in me. I want it to be absorbed. I take a shallow breath and I draw it up, I draw up my fear thought. As I breathe it out and up, I blow it out (like a whistle) before me in the Light reflection. It lies there and it shimmers and it is absorbed by the Light

> that cometh forth from the Image which is all good, all wondrous, all God's source. And in my mind's eye I see this being absorbed. Like a pool of water that it lies in, and this tremendous Sun is soaking it up. It is loved and blessed and caressed and purified. Then I give it a few moments and then I will draw that thought in, unto myself as a blessed, all good purified thought.
>
> I have drawn in the positive into my body and there it remains. So when next, another something of another nature happens I stop. Take a short breath and blow it out and lay it in the lovely pool with the Sun on it, I inhale it again bringing in the true reality, that it is healed, and pour it through my body, and say, "this is beautiful." And now the beauty lies in me.

A question was asked by a student whether 'do souls program or deliberately cause crises to come about in order to force the small self to get rid of ego and small distortions?' Fransesca responded:

> Yes and no. Went into this deeply at one time. If in earlier life we had known that our grandmother had-----and we must be so careful of that. We might not have been aware of it and could have put that in our minds and made a picture story. Then as we grow older they could add to it and say, 'Oh I hope I don't get that condition' which is one reason we have been so careful of not naming things. They are all a condition of inharmony in the body. Then we don't place them upon any organ.
>
> If we look backwards and we really want to know and understand properly which is good, because we are keeping

> active and we search, and then we have communion. Involuntarily we can say we are programmed. Or voluntarily we can program ourselves. There are people and I was one of them who said, 'Oh I can't get along on less than 10 or 12 hours of sleep or more.' Well I thought I couldn't get along on less than 10 or 12 hours. And suddenly I was tossed into the situation with Harry during the war years. People would come at 1, 2 or 3 a.m. for watch or glass repair. So suddenly I discovered, I am getting 5 or 4 hours of sleep and I adapted. So then I also programmed myself for less. So that's programming. That's why I had to say yes or no.

On January 26, 1981, Fransesca turned 77. Then there was another hospital stay in February of 1981 due to pneumonia. On February 22, 1981 she wrote a general letter and produced Newsletter number 18.

Fransesca didn't have anyone to go to for an answer to her spiritual questions. She had a mortal need for receiving answers. She:

> Knew that somewhere there had to be something... and something in me had to know about that 'something' and even if 199 times I was not quite certain of that SOMETHING, there was that ONE TIME when I absolutely positively unreservedly and whole heartedly KNEW that there was something and that I had touched that something and shaken hands with IT and felt ITS love and power and because of that once out of a thousand I was going to keep on fighting, teaching, finding, searching until the average was higher than that!

Fransesca had a deep empathy for others and could feel the feelings of another person. Compassion was greatly developed in her:

> He becomes his brother through compassion. When self gives itself up for great compassion to fellow brother – then it gives all it has and the compassion is a companion to love, then no restrictions...Think of union, compassion and love for all. She is her brother's keeper. Until she can come to her Brother in her own compassion towards him – she cannot come into possession of that greatest and most final gift of All – the God companion – Love!
>
> Fransesca spoke about the subject of weeping and said that:
>
> The humble weep for love (Master T.) This is different from emotional tears that have to do with the physical sense, or we wouldn't cry on the physical, mortal level. When we feel so deeply with our mind and our soul about something, that is a release, that is different.

Fransesca had a Master who made her go back in time to things that were bothering her. When she came upon one of these thoughts, a dozen thoughts along the same line would come to mind. She talked about them, trying to find forgiveness and asked for forgiveness from those she might have hurt.

It was amazing to find that many related subjects with other people came to light, from the storehouse of memory. It was not always easy for her but it was rewarding because the same things did not come to light to disturb Fransesca anymore for she had 'cleared' them. Fransesca 'cleared' throughout her life. She let go of pain, negatives and certain memories. She was a firm believer in externalizing frustrations and annoyances. She said,

"If we get annoyed, frustrated, or upset we work it out. Important to get the frustration out."

If someone is in pain she advised:

> This can cause a person to be worse than they were otherwise. In a sense yelling is one way of striking back – each one to their own.
>
> This manner or venting this upon something or at something. Try to feel compassion because someone is like that. Sometimes some people have inherited this trait in their nature and want to own someone – own others – own possessions – and not give up anything for anyone – it must be all theirs! Which of course is not the Happiness way. But they don't know that, so when they have to give up something (anything) it is PAINFUL. They feel cheated – empty – and in the back of their mind they might be saying 'well somebody has got to pay for this which I lost.'

Fransesca managed the physical pain in her leg well. She saw a chiropractor who also practiced acupuncture. Fransesca had a wonderful rapport with him and looked forward to these appointments. She also practised visualization techniques to help herself.

Fransesca grew stronger by various experiences in her life. This is not always the case for others:

> With some people trials and tragedies make them better persons because they can FEEL how it is for other people – and in time become stronger themselves. With others they merely 'give into it' and thus they crack up.

There are days when we flop – or think we FLOP but it also teaches us that we can GET UP AGAIN – which after all is then success! If I scold myself for 'flopping' then all I can say is that at least I RECOGNIZED that I 'flopped' and then I can tell myself 'well, you were pretty smart after all to RECOGNIZE that you were a dumb bunny yesterday' etc.

If we were 100% perfect there would be no use in our being here for there would be nothing to work TOWARDS.

We have to use different methods for different days. Some days the vehicle story works beautifully for me. Other days I have to go back to the naughty and good children in the body, etc. So certain picture stories come to mind and we use them – for you see if we stay with one type of picture, then it becomes monotonous, or no longer a play game – and we might tire of it, or the subconscious might think "oh, that's old stuff, I'm sick and tired of the same thing" ...so we find something to work for us.

But above all, we mustn't become discouraged or despise our SELF if we seemingly fail...After some 53 years of it I call upon any kind of resources to take me away from negatives, etc.

Chapter Twelve

Toronto

Fransesca had a favourite expression that she shared with many people: "Let your ears hear what your mouth is saying." Another phrase she taught was, "Don't let the outside inside. Let the inside outside." Her focus was always on the inner self, and having its qualities made manifest.

On January 21, 1981, Fransesca explained that when things go haywire, to picture oneself in Cosmic wave motion. Stand still and take a deep breath, or one can also sing a song for five minutes every hour. On this she explained:

> "Each soul must do their own awakening and reasoning it out:"
>
> We all have purposes – sometimes of brief duration with some, until we have FOUND OURSELVES, then suddenly the light dawns and we are grateful for even the few moments in time when someone showed they care – or at least we THOUGHT they did. Then out of all of this menagerie of human beings we find a 'someone' who is different

> – and we cherish that time with them. So it goes all through life. Cherish that which is good even if but for moments in time (weeks, months, years) as it all leads to another WAY – another choice 'someone' who is put into our path to serve. It is His way.

Fransesca had a favourite prayer entitled "Mustard Seed of Faith," a copy of which was placed in one's purse. Her sister gave it to Fransesca many years before when she was alone. She was always provided for and therefore had enough money to live on.

> Bless this billfold, Lord I pray,
> Replenish it from day to day,
> Give me faith, as a mustard seed,
> That I may harvest all I need.
> Help me earn and wisely spend
> Show me what to buy or lend, –
> Thank you Lord, for blessing me
> And sending me – Prosperity.
>
> Supply me now and evermore
> From thy vast abundant store.
> Amen.

The prayer must be used in sincerity and with the NEED for using it wisely – also to provide for Self in those ways of life which will be productive, useful – and also in sharing with others:

> I never spent it foolishly – for silly things – and always with the blessing thought that it could be shared – that it SHOULD be shared. I guess in the background also was the thought that I must WAIT until someone else wished

to pay for consultation – or classes, etc. not that I must ASK, for this is the TRUE MUSTARD SEED OF FAITH. The Biblical quotation is something like "and have ye the faith of a mustard seed?" – KNOWING that it will produce. If sharing this...it must be for a sacred purpose, with full respect to the Cosmic law.

Fransesca was also fond of a proverb, and referred to it in her teaching.

An Old Proverb

He who knows not – and
Knows that he know not – he's a fool
Shun him.

He who knows not
And knows that he knows not
He is ignorant – teach him.

He who knows and knows not that he knows –
He is asleep – wake him.

He who knows
And knows that he knows,
He is wise – follow him.

Fransesca believed in being assertive in life. "We have to be assertive and to believe in ourselves. Good to get mad at ourselves – that is healing." She had a technique for the formation of new habits and the breaking of old ones:

> List one habit that one would like to break and one that one would like to form. Direct one's wish as a command to the inner self. Need for this to be repetitive. Concentrate on one of these at a time and only once a habit pattern has been established. As soon as one has conquered something, then it becomes a habit.

Fransesca also had an exercise given for practicing visualization:

> ...Regarding an attunement with something one needs and wants. Create image of one thing. Live it. Blot out all other impressions. See oneself doing it in the now and having it in the now.
>
> Think of a situation one would like to have brought about. E.g. friendship with someone, harmony at home, greater popularity, more success, etc. Include oneself in the imagery, experiencing it already.

She also frequently discussed self-discipline. In attaining it, Fransesca taught that there were seven cardinal virtues:

1. Dedication (a decision)
2. Motivation (a commitment)
3. Willpower (the desire)
4. Persistence (the application)
5. Consistency (being steady, habitual)
6. Patience (attaining acceptance)
7. Expectancy (maintaining faith)

In a letter written on March 27, 1981, Fransesca wrote about the importance of proving ourselves to ourselves. She also mentioned moderation in all things. She started to decorate her stationary with pictures placed in the corners of each page containing images of nature, wildlife and flowers.

In a subsequent letter written on April 5, 1981, Fransesca again wrote about not overdoing any one specific thing:

> To clear takes STAMINA, courage, guts, good health, a sense of humour. If one is bringing up nasties so constantly – we become discouraged that we are not getting anywhere with it and will give up because we are bored, mad, etc. with a 'system': STOP for 2 nights and go into it again with a fresh viewpoint.

Fransesca worked on clearing the pictures made during the hospital stays:

> When we are trying to uncover or get rid of 'something' which isn't pretty, or nice to think about, the very fact that we are doing so – brings up more of the same, even things we had forgotten all about. When we ARE READY for this strict routine, we can surmount it eventually – but if we are FORCING ourselves into it, without that God-given motive behind us – it can also play havoc for the time being by bringing up other kinds of stuff we didn't expect to have come about.

Fransesca also mentioned meditation:

> In meditation, it is a good idea to avoid asking questions with a 'yes' or 'no' answer, as these are of the conscious self. Never ask a definite yes or no question. The Cosmic does not speak in words like a human voice. Cosmic speaks through symbols, signs, ideas. One can say for example, I

> am thinking of inquiring at... or I need to move, not 'shall I move?' Then one interprets the symbols received.

As Fransesca's health began to decline, she wrote:

> It appears I came to serve – and when NOT in service, life is not worthwhile or productive. It has therefore, never been easy for me to be 'served' – waited on – done for because I am a do-er and not a 'taker.'

At this time, Fransesca began to sort through tapes of recorded meditations and communions that she had. She said: "I go along with this business of getting the house in order."

The last letter Fransesca wrote to me was on May 5, 1981. She stated:

> You cannot step into the Channel of Good without great good immersing you and becoming blended by it. You could not step into the pure water (of Spirit) and have it touch your body, and walk onto shore – passing another person without leaving some drops of water upon them. Therefore, be watchful, that your feet (thoughts by which you move) and also actions are good.
>
> Always desire and pray and step within that good, good stream, not the murky or dark soil which might cling to or harm another.
>
> Do hurt to no one, knowingly. Ask forgiveness each night for any hurt done, known or unknown – FORGIVENESS may be given you also – when asked for. All things have two sides, there is no definite positive, nor negative – they must be balanced.

Fransesca used a technique for the body asking that "all cells be restored." She taught loving the body so that it becomes a conviction is vital. She said:

> Establish harmony. Do not state the condition or we accentuate the condition trying to get rid of. Otherwise, give power and energy to it. Ask for all cells in the body to be in harmony. Ask that there be contentment, peace, joy, love and ask that this be restored in oneself. See the cells as being whole – round and filled with energy.

Fransesca lived by this precept right unto the end of her life. "Thoughts are things" she taught. Therefore how one thinks was of prime importance:

> A person is as big as they think. Our thoughts determine our actions and our actions make one either prominent or small in a small, mental world.
>
> Have to have a love for knowledge. One may be intelligent and not educated or educated and not intelligent. Intelligence gives mind aptitude necessary to use what it has acquired.
>
> Each idea if it survives the test of experience has motif. There is no defeat except from within and only our weakness of purpose. The only dreamer who is worthless is the one who is just content to dream and allow his visions to dissipate. Must coordinate dream with reason and perception and incentive to action. Necessity is still the mother of invention.

Fransesca was practical and down to earth. She taught that:

There is no ungood, for everything is good at its source. Man makes it ungood and it goes forth and further away from source. Out of every ungood, good comes. We may not know the ungood at the time, but later it will be apparent.

Fransesca believed that everyone is good, until proven ungood. She also stated that emphasizing the good in oneself was something to be cultivated. Her Master said:

"There is no ungood – only all is good (God). Man, in retrospect will look backwards at what he saw once as ungood – then turn to his maker giving thanks to the GOOD which it has wrought. That good always follows when we see beyond the ungood."

It was exciting for Fransesca when another person actually responded and to know what she was talking about. She considered it to be a Cosmic reward. "Understanding is deeper and the soul chords have finally come alive, and are talking big and loud to you."

Fransesca believed that at bedtime it is a good idea to ask:

Did I walk in my own willful way today?
Did I wound a soul today?
Forgive.
Did I cause a foot to go astray today?

Also say,
I am at your service – use me and I will do Your will.

Say: Open my heart that I may give
Open my ears that I may hear
Open my eyes that I may see.

Give thanks for Cosmic presences in ones' life.

Fransesca's health continued to deteriorate in the last four months of her life. Fransesca traced her life into seventeen year cycles. Another seventeen-year cycle came to an end with Fransesca's death on July 13, 1981.

Chapter Thirteen

Suggestions

There were a number of suggestions, techniques and exercises recommended by Fransesca to undertake in one's spiritual practice. These were received during visits to her home and during talks between Fransesca and myself:

> Ask ourselves – what is our greatest priority? Then ask how am I going to accomplish it? What is or are the things which keep me from that? Only we can answer that for ourselves.
>
> It is a good idea to make a date with oneself to have spiritual reading or study time, for example, two evenings a month.
>
> Someone who agrees to discomfort and lets people walk all over them, is a habit that needs to be broken. That is conquering and it is Mastery.
>
> Can show humility to the Christ and for the Christ and face that Christ in one self and then we can stand up and be proud.

When we belittle ourselves, we belittle the Christ in us.

When we little by little remove some of the stumbling blocks, then we realize that we don't have big ones, only small ones.

Get a chisel and a hammer and in this corner and suddenly one finds that it's not a big rock at all. (when clearing).

It becomes a habit when one has a designated day and time for meditation – than one looks forward to it and one will feel renewed and rejuvenated.

We are given certain relatives in order to grow. If we were born into an uncomfortable situation, are we going to let this rule our life or are we going to rise above it a few steps?

God was willing to share his most precious possession – that is an unselfish love.

WE ARE A REFLECTION! And often we see in others the reflection of ourselves.

I am in God's Temple and God's spirit dwells in us.

Jesus said, 'No servant is greater than the Master nor is the Master greater than the servant.'

Actuality has act in it. When we have to realize something it has an ACTION on the physical plane and upon the body vehicle, so for that vehicle or entity it becomes an actualization.

From 3 to 5 in the morning is the very low point of physical vitality, the time of night when everyone else in the world is low – seem to direct their thoughts and feelings around the globe causing a low and negative vibe – not easy to dispel.

Our dream world is our thought world: is the world of the subconscious – we see and experience what we have fed into it.

Our names have an effect in vibration. Some consonants are stronger than others.

We are given what we are worthy to bear.

Thank the Cosmic for providing for us and for doing for us.

Accept what we have lovingly, gratefully and humbly in His way.

For every negative, replace it with a positive, for positive absorbs the negative. Replace it with what one loves more than anything else in the world.

Everything has its own space and time. Every situation needs to resolve itself.

We interpret a sign or a symbol as to where our consciousness is.

Yearn for the love of the Christ. Hunger and thirst for this.

Have an impersonal chord with someone handling a difficult situation.

Does one leave something of oneself which is good?

Bring sexual energy up the spine. See it as a narrow column of smoke. Bring it up to the third eye and purify it.

To increase circulation, pull hair away from scalp on either side of the head.

Watch the effects that different foods have on our body.

Respond to challenges by fighting back. Stand up to our convictions.

If something is stolen or missing, then send prayer to one who's got it, that it bring them joy and love, with which it went out. Ask a blessing upon it.

Reserve judgment. We don't always know what people are doing or what their past has been.

Accept beforehand a positive outcome when speaking to someone, giving a presentation, having a meeting, etc. Visualize the outcome as if it were happening in the present, then release it and let it go.

When one has a certain need and tried what one can do on the material plane, ask for special permission to petition the Cosmic. Always give thanks.

People must have a backbone.

Get anger out.

Know oneself as a consciousness.

The God within begets.

Our minds take pictures all the time of things that impress us deeply. In a quiet, subjective state, these pictures come forth.

When doing clearing (from within) do one item, because it brings up another grape cluster. Forgive, ask a blessing and LET GO!

Light a candle every time a beautiful thing happens.

Take one thing for a week, one subject at a time. One thing that bothers one. Do spiritual fasting for five minutes out of every hour. Example procrastination, jealousy, fear of being poor. Ask for forgiveness and a blessing also. We want to get rid of __________ and be forgiven for_________.

Seal one's consciousness of all negativity.

Be mistress of one's home.

Ask that one's Light so shine.

Are we looking at everything from His level or from the level of a garbage can? We identify with all things and with all people.

Do things for another.

Love teaches obedience.

Cosmically necessary that we complete the tasks we have come to do.

Must be an example of what you believe.

Cosmic love in man is man's strength. It is NOT his weakness.

Love begets love.

Have Higher Self rule, lead, reach and become the whole self.

Being on the Path requires discipline and upmost dedication. When the Master asks to drink of the cup, it takes courage and love for all. There is no turning back. Don't say yes unless you are willing to give up your own desires for everyone and anyone!

There is no phenomenon which is separate from the whole spectrum of Cosmic reality and law. Attachment must be acquired through personal study of basic laws and principles.

Cosmic memory self is in contact with Higher Self, which in turn is in touch with Divine Mind.

When faced with an uncomfortable situation...if we can 'assume' another 'attitude' towards an unfavourable situation – will see something we missed before – the change in our attitude will help us. Ask yourself "what is my present attitude towards ______? Ask 'how can I change it?' You can't change person x but you <u>can</u> change how or why one responds adversely. This will help one grow."

The following prayer can be used daily:
The Light of the Christ is in and around me
Nothing but good may come unto me
Nothing but good may go forth from me.
I give thanks. I give thanks. I give thanks.

Ask inner self for help with decisions. (May be a visual image, subtle urge or voice)

It is important to drink water. It is also a good idea to have a bowl of water in each room to absorb negativity.

Usually the natal day is a good day to have one's meditation and communion time. Keep this day special, when not available to others.

We must be an example. An example of Christ. Fishers of men – draw others into the net.

Eternal love is that which is real love. It is remembered again and again and again. The same first feeling always comes back.

Avoid dissecting the soul.

Give thanks for the hardest of times.

When we hold other people in judgment, we are not truly forgiving them.

We are the creator of formings. Be careful of what one creates.

Turn on a beam of Light to a problem, to people and places.

See the cells in the body being happy and open.

Each day arouse greater emotions.

Love always remembers.

Don't bite off more than you can chew.

We came to serve and to be examples. When serving people – see what they can really accomplish.

A true channel is a channel of love.

Each person has his/her own path to follow.

Divine form impresses itself through a channel.

Love energy can be felt and observed.

The way of the Ego is the unnatural way. The way of the Master is the NATURAL WAY.

Although dictated by Amhadra on October 18 1954, "The Ten Commandments," are timeless in nature:

The Ten Commandments

Be still – in order to hear Him speak.

Re Reverent – of all His works, thro whomever they may come.

Be humble – with LOVING humility.

Be SELF-LESS not SELF-FULL!

Be faithful to your Work – which is His work.

Be of Open Mind, allowing open mind to others which is God's Free Will.

Be EXPECTANT and joyful in spiritual contacts and communion, for it is of GOD.

BE EVER ready to give – as well as receive, for it is HE who gives, and you receive thro Him.

Be PATIENT; serene, gentle and not boastful.

BE ALWAYS grateful to the source from whence springeth Thy strength.

All these which you do – will bring thousand fold these same to you. In aid – in love – because they ARE all OF GOD also!

Fransesca wrote The Beatitudes for her first spiritual daughter, Irene. They were dictated by Amhadra.

The Beatitudes

Book learning is physical intelligence.

Heart learning – is God – in – action.

Spoken words without thought – are wasted God-energy.

Thoughts with positive directedness – are well used God Power.

Positively directed thoughts, return with dividends like unto themselves.

Negative thoughts are scattered, thereby returning scattered dividends.

Desiring for Self, and Self alone, closes the horizon to Self Only.

Desiring FOR Self – to give for OTHERS, enlarges the scope so that FROM others His source may also come to you – and yours blend and go unto them.

Appendices

Appendix I

Christ Mass – All Glory Be Thine!

Christmas in Michigan!!! – of 'way back Half Past Six – was breathtakingly lovely – in the long ago crispy night. Candle lit windows cast shadowy highlights over the new snow as I trudged my way homeward. Tracks of my sled were obliterated within the instant! I ran as fast as my numbed feet would take me – to reach the market – but the flickering lights of "SCHULTZ – MEATS – GROCERIES AND SUNDRIES" – was a welcome sight. Old John Schultz was the proud possessor of the first gas lighted sign our neighbourhood had seen – but on this blowy snow laden night, the words were distorted into a blur of half letters.

WHAT a store!!!...huge iron stove – fired with coal, held the place of honour in centre aisle...apple boxes and rickety rocker were resting places for the regular customers. Odor of shiny red apples...blended with fragrance of briny pickles – and crocks of sauerkraut – right near the pretzels with invitation for "just a taste" was more than my hungry tummy could stand.

Low glass show case – just right for the small ones – tempted me with its array of sugared treats...a 'speshul' section of 'five for a penny' was finger marked by grimy little paws...long licorice sticks, horehound drops...jelly beans of enormous size... home made suckers...fruit centered hard 'balls' (a bag full for two pennies) and 'taster-treats' for the 'speshul' customers of age

UNDER seven...was the bargaining spot for the neighbourhood small fry. (Ah, to never be beyond SEVEN!!!)

Old Mr. John crippled with lumbago, came in from the back sitting room, creaking and thumping on his one good leg – always ready to "sit a spell' and listen to the joys or woes of his customers – or offer advice. He was the neighbourhood counselor, wise, witty, and OH so SHARP with a bargain! His kind have departed with the age of the 'Super-this and super-duper that"!

What luxury!!!...what precious memories!!! – no need to hurry...no long lines of grocery carts...no pressures...no 'zippo' service – always enough time to ask about my lessons, the new beau – my teacher – that fatal report card – or to be my confidant in a cherished childish 'secrut.' My shopping completed he gave me a gaudy advertising tie rack (as was his custom), to each steady customer of his market.

My! MY! thought I (almost seven), 'what will papa do with all of them? I had collected six racks from various stores of my special selection!!)

Tinga-ling-ling, announced another late shopper, and the blast of cold air chilled yet delighted me when the door opened. THIS WAS Christmas time indeed!

With a garbled, "Thank you Mr. John for the present, Merry christmas to you see you pretty soon, I gott a hurry, Santa's coming to night, goodbye!" I slammed the door.

OoooHHohhhhH – huge snowflakes! Like stars!!! They clung to my lashes, and with my cross eyed attempt to see them more clearly they appeared very funny indeed! Red knitted stocking cap and mittens were powdery white before I reached the house. Snow swirled about in a happy mood – white and fluffy and so crunchy crisp!! (uhhh uhhhhhh – how fine it 'tis to be 'most seven!)

'Round to the woodshed with my snow laden sled – I brushed it off REAL good, 'cuz THIS WAS Christmas! Wouldn't dare be forgetful on this night of all nights! NO SIR! Not with Santa peeking in every window!! Brr – I shivered – it's cold, but 'gotta get this done right, 'cuz he might not leave me any 'presunts.' It's been kinda hard to be good for such a long long time (about two weeks), – wouldn't want to spoil things now! Not me – no sir ree, not me!" The small black porch leading to the kitchen was lined with hooks for those under seven – hooks for everything from cap to rubbers! "Yes sir, yes man – everything in its place – mama isn't going to catch me this night with, "brush the snow off your coat!!!...hang up your cap...shake your scarf...did you leave your mittens again?...put your rubbers on the paper...wipe your feet...where have you been?...did you do what I told you to?" Oh yes mama, I 'tended to it all right, real good I did!"

Yumm mmm, mama looked so warm and inviting when I rushed to her with my 'presunt.' Her tiny body was just the right size to love – so soft and warm – very very comforting to one 'just six' almost seven! Hurrying to the huge kitchen range to warm my hands, there as always were my slippers, toasty warm on the rack beside it. WHAT memories! (how many thousand times have our feet been blessed with the warmth of this special attention of love by one little mother!)

When she opened the oven door I peeked ...uuuhh – OH! – a large goose was brown and crisp, just begging to be adorned with very special apples...and the ducks in the roaster nearby frowned at the honour of being shown their neighbour. Shivers of anticipation raced up my spine...why was it so long 'for supper? Bubbling pots of vegetables and 'taters covered the oven top...the fire pot almost red hot to hasten the oven browning...

yeast rolls covered with yellow cloth waited patiently for their turn. A long wall table, built by papa, overflowed with delicious samples of mama's baking artistry – Streusel kuchen, miniature fancy pastries, apple. pumpkin and lemon pies, cookies of every variety and shape, gingerbread men, pheffernusse, peanut squares, coconut crunchies, sugar cookies, cut-outs, – decorated in red and green sugars...a five layer yellow butter cake – and ah....- the mostest, mostest 'speshul' (to age Six, nearly seven), the moist poppy seed cake, Special Delivery Direct from Heaven. I drooled whilst one finger surreptitiously found its way into the creamy frosting for one stealthy forbidden lick!

On this festive night, we had our supper in the dining room, beautifully decorated with pine boughs, silver bells and red ribbons. Wreaths and garlands were in every window – and the snowy white curtains blended with the white linen supper cloth. Holly berry clusters were tacked to each corner of the cloth and small pine segments were pinned beside each place setting!

A gas chandelier – sparkling with variated glass encrustations, was lowered for this night – and on Christs' night, it was turned up BRIGHT! Large coal base burner stove, cast a crimson red glow through the isinglass of its fire door, and it crackled and spit as the wind roared down the chimney. My toes wiggled in sheer delight! Every sound on the deserted street was magnified, – and wind blown snow from the caves bristled as they fell on the porch with a thump! HOW WONDERFUL!!!! – how EXCITING! – how exhilarating to be Half Past Six!!

Musical sound of sleighbells in the distance – and the slow trot-trot of horses pulling their sleighs seemed like the sound of heralding angels going forth to proclaim this night. Mr. Schultz would soon be out in his sleigh too – playing Angel-Santa to the needy families on his route. Dear Old John!!

The wee, ee-ee-pftt, pftt, pftt, puff-puffpuff of the street car was delightful as old Myrtle croaked and lumbered painfully down the icy tracks! No speed demon was old Myrtle – she came slowly down our block, like lavender and old lace, stopping in front of our house – in the MIDDLE of the block! Big Frank, the conductor, diga-linged his whistle! Little Mama rushed out – without sweater or coat to hand him his basket of Christmas cheer. She NEVER forgot – 'cuz once he rescued my puppy from beside the tracks!

AT LAST! SUPPER! Bowed heads....silent prayer...crackling stove...enticing odors of every good thing before us...love in abundance...truly lifted the Christ high within us – this blessed night!

Somehow Santa Claus and Christ were mixed up together in my mind. "Which one was Christ?...I felt he must be Santa Claus – because He was so very good. It was SO simple to love Him, 'cuz He was just real easy for 'enybuddy' to love. I 'spected that all children were good – just 'cuz of Him! (only not me always!!) In my childish mind the baby Jesus was like a Baby Santa Claus, who grew up and got bigger – and bigger – and bigger – and all the time He kept on being 'good' and 'gooder' and loving more and more, and giving and giving, and people just received Him in their homes and called Him, "Santa Claus." He ALWAYS knew what little children wanted! He knew what the big folks wanted too – but they didn't always accept what He gave them...but most 'little kids' did, 'cuz they were pretty close to Santa Claus who was "HIM." So I figured it out real simple, when I was just half past six. The little baby Jesus was very dear to me – He was just the real spirit of Christmas, and when He became bigger and bigger and bigger – he became Christ – from out of the little baby Jesus, and He'd come to my house to call too – but yet other people just called Him, 'Santa Claus' to sorta represent Him.

I looked round the table and wondered if mama and papa understood this real good like I did – and I figured inside myself, that some day I would ask them about it, but inside of myself, I knew this was REAL 'cuz it was just like He had told it to me when I was very, very little, 'not quite five.' Somehow I remember how He came to live with me – and when I got 'scairt' or was hurt or sumpin' – and it was Oh so dark and alone in my big room upstairs, I would lay my head on my pillow and talk to a little baby-Jesus, 'cuz that was very easy to do, 'cuz He was little just like me.

I used to hope when I was SMALL (not quite five) – that perhaps I could grow up like Him and maybe be kinda like a 'presentative' of Him, and be a Lady Santa-Claus or like a big sister of the baby Jesus who grew up. While my mama and papa were saying their silent prayer, I was a-thinkin' and a-thinkin' all this by myself, and being very glad that now that I was bigger, 'most seven, – that I knew about things like that!!!

THEN! Papa pushed back his chair, and standing proud and happy before us, he toasted this Night, with a glass of rich grape wine! I toasted too, with a tiny glass of diluted juice – first to the Night – the spirit of its' message – to the year just past, and the one ahead – to each other – and to Love!

Mama heaped my plate with just 'so much' of this, and 'so much' of that, saying, "Your eyes are bigger than your stomach – when this is finished you may have some more!" Ah – the training of childhood has remained the rule of a life time, "Never waste – because others might be hungry...be generous – but also frugal." Her words still ring in my heart – as does the sound of her loving voice!

Brother and sister, so VERY old (nearly 17 and 18) teased each other about their dates, and brothers' mimicry of sisters' beaus brought a blush to her cheeks! I thought they were very very funny....gee! – they seemed to not even think about Santa Claus at all!...only 'fellers and girls' and dancing and dates! My goodness! Wasn't anybuddy interested in Him – but me?!!

'Pass the dressing...pass the gravy...where's the yams?...I'd like some duck – no, that piece is too much, give me the little one over there...here! Here! You can't lift the plate it's too heavy... ohhhh, it's hot! – NOW look what you've done you've dribbled on your new apron!...DON'T eat so fast – we have lots of time, chew your food, not such BIG mouthfuls ...eat your salad it's the kind you like...NO! you can't go skating tomorrow, we're having company for Christmas dinner. The turkey is stuffed and ready for tomorrow!!!

I groaned. TURKEY TOMORROW?? – with the ducks and plump goose before me – and apple pie, pumkin too, butter cake, poppy cake with the Angel-from-heaven-sauce? WHO could POSSIBLY eat tomorrow? Surely I would never, never, NEVER be able to eat again! Mother beamed...happy as a loving German housefrau when her family is well fed. She had no time for eating, she was too busy serving...but her food was the joy of a full heart!

Mama's long starchy apron made swish-swish sounds as she cleared the table. Wood range burbled noisily – the water well spurted and hissed with its steaming water. It seemed to me that EVERYONE conspired to extend the clean up process as long as possible. There was no end to this Christmas Eve suspense. The Parlor Door had been closed to us for 48 hours, not even papa could set foot in this room of many secrets – for it was Mama's private domain (Santa's helper).

Then – like a major domo, our vivacious little mama ordered us upstairs – one by one. "Upstairs! All of you – quickly – Santa Claus is coming! Hurry!" Papa tried to sneak to the rocker behind the roaring stove, stuffing his pipe, and preparing to place his stocking feet against the lower belly of the baseburner. Mama's eagle eye caught the truant, and sent him upstairs "with the children." Poor Papa! Never once did he get away with it – although he always tried. But he went because he loved the little mama with a holy adoration!!

Ooohhhh – it was cold upstairs! The only heating came from the floor register which captured the warmth of the dining room base burner, and the floor grating was a very inviting place. It was 'speshully so for Half Past Six, as I lay on my tummy to peek through the grate to figure what mama was doing downstairs. Couldn't see very well though, – for mama knew all about little girls and had closed the grating!! AT LAST! The moment had arrived! – yet we dared not go downstairs 'till mama summoned us.

At the foot of the long stairway stood the God loved little mother, cupping her hands to her mouth she trumpeted, 'toota-roo-tootarah-toota-roo-toot! Santa Claus has come toota-roo-too!" Papa led the way down those 28 long steps – and in all the world of worlds, never NEVER was there such a sight!!

The gas light had been extinguished, and the cherry glow flickering thro isinglass of the baseburner, was our only light. We stood in a row before the archway to the Parlor – and THERE! – surely the Christ-Santa-Claus had been!

The far wall was graced by a perfect pine tree, its golden star touched the ceiling and each branch blazed with lighted miniature candles (REAL ONES) in every variation of color! Boughs were laden with ornaments from Germany – cranberry strings, decorations which we had made in our cozy winter nights, – so we could give something of 'ourselves' to Him. The candles flickered with our movement, and the warmth of their flame brought out the spicy odor of the pine needles. But!! – there is MORE – for a heart can only stand one cupful of beauty at a glance.

In separated places, around the walls of the Parlor were five small tables, – covered with a white cloth dropping to the floor. EVERY table held a dish of fruit – large oranges, apples and grapes (a real luxury) – a dish of figs, nuts and raisins (A Christmas delight) – a plate of homemade candy – but ah – the most GLORIOUS of all glories, a TREE! In the center of each table, which bore our name was a miniature Xmas tree – fresh from the forest, NO artificial tree was this, nor manufactured coloring, – but fragrant and pungent in its small stand of water! FIVE candle lit small trees (one for each one of us), five tables heaped with fruits and surrounded at their base with our gifts... and the Crowning Big Tree, the father and mother of them all! Was there ever such a Christmas in the whole wide world? My eyes of 'many times seven' fill with tears even now at these precious memories of love.

Hand in hand, little mama led us into the parlor and placed before our own private Tree-table. Before we could peek at our gifts, she led us with "Stille Naht, Heiliger Naht (Silent Night, Holy Night), – then – with a gesture, she motioned us to our gifts! Papers flew – ribbons were unfurled – shouts, cries – tears – laughter, excitement – happiness! Joy over the simplest things....'a furry 'tassle' cap (what every young woman should wear at half past six)...crayons...a pencil box, was ANYONE ever so rich as 'just six, nearly seven?

"Thank you Mama, thank you papa, thank you sister, thank you brother, thank you Santa Claus Jesus, thank you everybody!" kissing, hugging, shouting, tears and laughter were all mixed up with one another. Dear little mama just stood in the doorway, hands across her tummy – beaming. She had forgotten her own table in the joy of watching our excitement! When it came her turn she always said, "it was 'zactly what I wanted." There were NO gifts to be exchanged, no complaints, no disparaging remarks, no comparison of 'what others may have' just love and love and the joy of giving and receiving THANKFULLY whatever was given!!

Papa comfy in the rocker, decked out in the new 'smoking jacket' and felt slippers smoked and talked, and told stories of Christmases in the 'old country.' Warm, cozy, homey, loving comforting and so cherished, were the simple Christmases of this Home of Love. You ask, "Is this a Christmas Editorial? – and a story of Christ's birth? Yes – ah yes – indeed it is!!

He was born and re-born – born and re-born, day after day, year after year, hour upon hour, through love manifesting itself in every manner, in this Home of His love Christ in Christmas??? Yes, oh yes yes!

Where has the Christmas Christ disappeared to in these modern days of hurry? What has happened to the 'old' Christ Mass, when he lived in the kitchen, and came to dinner? When He was born before the candlelit Christ Tree – when He was wrapped within the tissue wrappings,

Ah yes –

Was not Christ in all this giving –
Who came to call and was Living?
Did He not sit – before our table?
And bless the food and every ladle?

Was not He present, when family gathered,
In the Love Lit House, where naught else mattered?
Isn't CHRIST – Christmas – the Giver and giving

And not materiality – of the gift of its' ribbon?
Did not He arrive when Mr. Claus came –
And walk amongst men – as "Santa' in Name?
Was not the real Santa – His mortal-life image
Of that Holy One of the Christ child fame?
Does not He come calling, in strife or in trouble?
And quicken your love – if you know His name?
Or does He come wrapped in tinsel and glitter?
With price tags and thoughts, of the 'present gained."
Yet to the small child of Six – 'most Seven'
She KNEW that He came – as the Love of her heaven,
For only in Love, can He come yet again
As Love bringeth peace and good will to all men.

My story so simple, from long, long ago,
Was true at Age Seven or a hundred or more,
He came then to bless – in Santa- Claus Love –
But still He was Christ ---YES really He WAS!

With tear dimmed eyes and a sob in my throat, I share a Christ Mass which from Age Six ('most Seven) was duplicated throughout my life. Every word is true – each one like a golden chain linking Love to Love – from the Garland of Flowers of His Heart.

Appendix II

The following Treatise was dictated by Master T. when Fransesca lived in San Jose.

INTRODUCTION

The discourses which follow, are instructive in nature, written in a simple style, and progressive in their explanations. They have been received from the Master T. under whose tutelage the Transcriber has been for many cycles.

The purpose of our instruction is for eventual Soul-Realization – one of the holiest events in mortal life. It is available to any student who pauses on each Step of the Path – in meditation and application of the principles outlined. Each discourse is complete within itself – in accordance with the Series in which it is bound. Esoteric explanations will follow in later series in a sequential manner.

The progression of the Ego will be self evident – according to the study and perseverance given on each Step of the Way. In our association with students on the Path, this system of mental regimentation has increased their psychic and spiritual powers. That Pearl of Great Price so fervently sought for through the Ages, is possible of attainment, and his Door is open to all. Results WILL be obtained by the Seeker who walks THROUGH the doorway – and deliberates on each step of this Path.

The procedure given in each classification of our study is that which the Transcriber has tested, under personal training with the beloved Master T. Every aspect outlined in these Series has been vouched for through personal experimentation and proven workable.

It will be our pleasure to assist any of our students with problems they might encounter – as it would defeat our purpose of unification and integration of the Whole Self, if points of discussion were not completely understood. Each subject has many ramifications and side branches, which could not be included in a work of this nature – but a basic foundation is given to assist the Seeker in his goal towards Illumination. The personality structure and adaptability of each neophyte is not identical in nature – therefore personal problems will arise, which we shall be pleased to assist you with.

It is our contention that spiritual instruction should not be laborious or tedious – rather a period of quiet joy and anticipation of the approaching study hour. It should be a happy adventure in the Schoolroom – waiting for the instruction of the Master. However – the neophyte must make that first Step upon the Path, with earnestness of purpose, diligence and patience – to be worthy of this Cosmic honor.

We pray that you will find Him within yourself – or at your side, and be glorified in the peace which this union brings. This relationship IS possible for the sincere Seeker – who has that courage, humility of heart and spirit, to approach the Step – walk through the Door – and sit quietly at His feet and listen.

It is my humble honor to serve as the Instrument and Transcriber for the Beloved Master T.

Fransesca

"The Lord is good unto them that wait for him, to the soul that seeketh him.: – Lamentations 3:25

"Behold, I stand at the door, and knock: if any man hear my voice and opens the door, I will come in to him, and will sup with him and he will with me." Rev. 3:20

TREATISE

Part One

CONTENTS

Master T. has recommended that this Treatise be read through completely. Thereafter, the student is requested to study each Part of the Way – ONE step at a time for at least a period of one month – applying the Steps until they have been conquered...

The initial effort towards integration of finite and infinite Mind catapults the Seeker at the feet of his first formidable adversary – the Ogre Concentration!

The metaphysical quest is begun with exalted purpose – determination and enthusiasm. You are POSITIVE that in your enthusiastic and confident state of mind, every obstacle on the path to your desire will be overcome. There will be NO diminution of YOUR efforts on the road to Mastership!!!! (Ah – Small One! How confident thou art in the beginning!)

Follow us now, as we eavesdrop on Little Joe – in his methodical preparations for his first concentration period. He moves his chair to position – just so – arranges the candles and incense on his altar and lights them with care. He smiles towards the floral offering which he has placed beside them, pleased with himself, in having attended to each detail of his Book of Instruction! His rambling thoughts, a composite of many eager students is interesting to relate. "I wonder if the book said to put the incense above – or below my eye level? – humm, – no, I'll move it. – there, that's better. Oh – I guess I ought to pray – maybe a few deep breaths will help." (puff, puff) – (Ah, relax, Joe, relax) Silence for a moment. (We must smile as his gaze moves about the room). – Hmmm that picture is crooked again – I'll have to do something about that – now oh, where was I? Oh yes, I was concentrating. Now – I wonder what I am supposed to concentrate on? Maybe if I just stare straight ahead like they said, it will keep my mind occupied." – Silence – silence – then, "oh, that starting makes my eyes burn, – now they're watering- – I wonder if that's all right – they didn't say anything about that." – pause. Pause – Well – I guess I'll look someplace else – m m mmm, – maybe I should close my eyes. No, – better not – I almost fell asleep. ---- well the book said to blink several times – that'll fix it! Pause. Pause – "wonder if I turned off the water before I sat down? – sounds like a car – hope we're not having company, – just when I'm starting to concentrate so well – no – they moved on." – Silence – uneasy movements of the body – restless hands – poor Joe doesn't know what to do with them – Ah – in our observations we recognize the sign – yes, here it comes: – "Well – I think I have sat long enough today and concentrated. Nothing much happened, but I'll try again tomorrow. Anyway, my eyes smarted, that ought to mean something, but I don't know just what."

This – dear friends – is NOT a caricature of the Concentration processes of the minority – it is repeated daily in its many forms, by those who struggle with the first step – the gateway to eventual Cosmic realization. Invariably, after a few dozen unsuccessful attempts the periods are decreased, and soon they have ceased. WHY? Because Little Joe, our Conqueror, did not have the intestinal fortitude to continue the regime of marshalling the thought forces or persevering until he had conquered that first step towards Soul Realization.

If we were to follow our fictitious Joe-Personality through the succeeding months or years of his life, we would find the pattern holding true to form. The "habit" of procrastination would be evident in every facet of his life, and the promises to himself (or others) would be as incipient as his endeavors. Joe, although a Seeker at heart – desirous of Cosmic illumination will remain like all others of his kind, who skim through every Garden of Knowledge for some easier manner of embracing the Great Whit Throne!

With complete sincerity we must confess that there is NO WAY – or no course on "how to Become a Master in Six Easy Lessons" which can justify such a statement. Spiritual enlightenment, or Cosmic Consciousness can only shed their glory, through the route of perseverance – practice, practice, practice with steadfastness of purpose. The harmony and rhythm of the Cosmic Universe and it's earth Satellite are dependent upon the natural functioning of every material and spiritual law. There is NO deviation from this Law and Order!

Consequently there is no law which operates as a side issue for a chosen few – and neglects all others. If this were the case, the System of His Rule and Order would collapse. If you have been deluded into believing a rapid method of unfoldment could be yours – WITHOUT effort on your part – then Beloved Ones, slumber on – until the New Awakening. It CANNOT BE!

Every gestation, whether animal, vegetable or mineral follows it's natural pattern, a series of sequences according to the law of the cycle, and the existence of this law and Order brooks no interference. The Egoic evolution is under the natural law of sequences. When the natural and harmonious pattern is followed in its stages of Becoming, the personality is balanced – projects its noblest qualities of the interlaced dual Ego.

We admit that there are methods of awakening certain psychic centers (plexuses) through stimulation, but we discourage this practice, – unless it is under the personal supervision of a Cosmic Master – who is aware of the three fold nature of his disciple – and the cosmic pattern. Self experimentation in this field is an interference with the Divine Order – and will result in an imbalance of the Personality. (Let there be peace between He and Thee!)

The sixteenth letter of the alphabet contains Power Words – which WILL produce spiritual results – i.e. Patience – Perseverance – Passivity – Prayer – Purity (of) Purpose – Positive approach – Polarity result – Progress Principle – Pride – Praise – Practice – Proof – Psychic Perception – and many more! With the ideal of the sixteenth letter and its innumerable companions, every door to His Kingdom can be opened. NOTHING is impossible between He and Thee!

We contend that NO seeker will fail to attain their quota of spiritual wealth of His realm, if they follow the precepts of the sixteenth letter – in their Egoic explorations. Failure is IMPOSSIBLE! – if you persevere. Patience and Perseverance must become the handmaidens in the normality of living, – a habit formed early on the Roadway to the Light! There is no success through sporadic endeavors – or the weak approach of, "when I have more time I will do it." The Ladder at this point is very shaky under the feet of the trembling Seeker. If you desire to see the Star – you MUST keep your eyes open long enough to behold its glory.

Our discourses are in simple style, exempt from vague illusions or abstract considerations. It is our contention that the greatest truths are those which are spoken in words familiar to the consciousness, and simple for mental digestion. Reading, learning, studying, applying, – should be a joyous event. The period of conversation with the Instructor, whether in or out of the body – should be a happy association – each day providing its own advancement, – full of exciting adventure into the Known and Unknown Realm. Let us enter therein NOW.

Concentration Vs. Meditation

The words "concentration and meditation" have been used interchangeably, – although there is a distinguishing line in their demonstration and application. The former is the act of focusing the attention – through mental powers and energies, upon ONE subject, object or thing. Meditation, on the other hand, is the utilization of this same concentration – directed towards Realization of God – becoming one with Him – within the Self. Concentration therefore, is the Outer manifestation – or its objective form. Meditation is that same concentration directed inwards, in its subjective and spiritual aspect.

In your world of externalities the dissipation of constructive energies are sacrificial offerings to the altar of Idle Thought. (Little Joe sways between me and thee and thee).

The brain cells contain your greatest powers. This power is depleted through careless thought which scatters its force in all directions – without the directive control of this powerful vibrational thought energy. When it is harnessed in one glorious Powerhouse of Control – you have access to the unlimited resources of the mighty Ocean of Infinity.

It has been said that the brain cells of mortal provide him with the unbelievable total of millions and trillions of electrical sparklers – who activate the living body. Yet – only a small portion of these are ever utilized by the average man! Is it not therefore conceivable to the Thinker, that there are NO limitations for the extension of this Atomic Powerhouse in himself? PERSEVERANCE stimulates – and prods – awakens – motivates – cell upon cell in their actions. You have been given the most magnificent equipment in the world of animal, vegetable or mineral! An unobstructed Fairyland is available to you when you stimulate the activity in each Chamber of your Powerhouse. ("In my Father's House are Many Mansions.") Mental stimulation – prodings – questionings – WILL produce results. The Genii of Alladin's lamp will be the Master of your endeavors. His Mind will be the Magic Carpet – and your brain the Garden Spot on which He will deposit His Treasures! Do you have the Patience and Powerful determination to witness your own transformation? Are you able to withstand the vibrations of higher mind – when He reveals Himself in you? Then dear ones, persevere as we lead you gently and firmly – along the Path.

Concentration may be likened to a Cosmic radiation – which has the power to burn (through a high powered frequency) – to move through – break open – separate – or unite with another force of equal intensity. The old story so often utilized to demonstrate this point is, of the sheet of paper on which sunrays are directed through a magnifying glass. The directiveness and power of their beam eventually burns a hole in the paper. This is a simple illustration of true concentration.

Intensity of concentration – and one-pointedness of purpose, is accomplished through Will – and reasoning powers of Conscious mind. Therefore – positive power on the material plane is generated – and its action MUST produce results. Another group of cells, lying dormant in the Powerhouse announce themselves to the World of Brain with joy, "I am alive – I am functioning – and I too am a part of this body in which I have been housed." There is NO danger of depleting the brainpower – as in the normal individual only a small portion of this tremendous radiating energy is utilized. If you desire to be a true Light in the World – then the flame in your brain must become activated, in order that it can be a proper field of force for the Power Reception of Higher Minds! In later discourses we will express ourselves on the esoteric meaning of the True Light of the World! The story handed down through the ages by the Hindu sages demonstrates the reality of true concentration.

A beloved Master was in earnest conversation with his disciple. During the master's summary in the morning's lesson, he found his Young One mentally wandering in thought. His attention was divided between the rustling sounds of the forest, the movement in the branches, – and interest in the young buffalo grazing nearby. He reprimanded the Young One – who replied, "But Master – I find it very difficult to confine my attention to your discourse this morning, – the actions of the buffalo interest me – and the sounds in the forest amuse me." This was the moment for exemplifying the lesson on Concentration. "My son – you shall learn your lesson through a demonstration. This morning you will enter the Silence Chamber with your Buffalo – and while you are with him, you shall study his actions and learn everything there is to know about the animal."

The following morning he looked through the window of the Silence Chamber and saw the Young One in studious concentration. "What have you learnt about the buffalo?" he questioned. "I have studied the movements carefully, and I am now able to walk like him. May we come out now?" But the Wise Master told his disciple that he had not yet learnt the entire lesson. Several days later he looked into the Silence Chamber again, – and discovered the Young One walking on all fours, making sounds like the buffalo. He again asked him the same question, and the Young One replied: "I have learnt to walk like my buffalo – I can bellow like he does, and I feel within me his ferociousness. May we leave the Chamber now?" "No, not yet, my son, you have not completed the study, – go deeper." On the sixth morning, he spoke with him again "How is it with you this morning, My Son. Have you found the answer?" Proudly the Young One answered, "I am NOT your Son, I AM the buffalo!"

The moral of the story is – that through his one-pointedness of concentration, the Young One became ONE with the object of his thought! He had identified himself with the Animal, through the power of observation and will – to the exclusion of any other objective! This is a classic example of the constructive directive power of mind. There is nothing impossible of attainment when the student has learnt subjugation of the wandering thoughts – and harnessed his power on <u>one</u>.

Concentration should be entered into for a definite purpose: a specific goal – desire – question – knowledge – clarification – enlightenment – assistance for Self – or others. The "Silence Chamber" of your concentration period should be a place in which you are assured of a modicum of privacy. You should be inspired with good intentions and sincere in your efforts to be patient until you succeed. Your one thought for the period of concentration should be mentally placed before yourself, as though you had written it on paper and fastened it to a screen before you, which you could read your thought. We speak of this process, as "writing in mind – with the fingers of thought." Only ONE thought – (written in mind), should be brought to the Table of the Lord, during the period you have chosen for concentration! If you restrain yourself to this one-pointedness the first battle as a Conqueror will be accomplished. At the close of this lesson a method of entering into this period will be given.

At this point in our discourse Little Joe enters our story once more. He has read the lesson to this point, and nods his head in consternation. We must smile with him, as we hear his mental observations. "Oh sure, everyone tells me to concentrate to think of only one thing at a time!!! – but I don't believe it can be done! – I ought to know – because I have tried!!! – Every time I sit down and decide that I won't think about anything, every sort of thought comes into my mind that I don't want there – every annoyance I can conceive of happens just when I don't want it to! NO one can tell ME that it is easy to concentrate and not – think."

Yes, dear friends, our Little Joe has told the same sad tale which has been heard from age to age, in one form or another. As you read these words you find yourself agreeing with Little Joe.

Be patient – your time will come! When the first hurdle has been vanquished you will find yourself in the condition of serenity – and the state of "NO THOUGHT." This is the "place" of golden, vibrant and glowing Silence. Later you will wonder where "thought" is – or has gone to – and what has happened to the Noise of the Mind with its ceaseless demands. You say, "impossible?" – We reassure you – 'not only possible, but most probable!"

While it is true, that the pathway to the Doorway of Thought, and its one pointed directiveness is not an easy one, it CAN be accomplished with considerable success, by any student who will give a small portion of each day to this gainful purpose. In this present cycle, much of man's "thinking" has been done for him by others. Humankind finds it simpler to follow the lines of least resistance, – reading what others have "thought through" – enjoying novels which take no effort, or training of the mind, to comprehend. The actions and characterizations of the Personalities in the novels have all been thought out by the author – and the reader does not need to activate brain cells in an effort to forecast the climax or conclusion of the story. The problem of thinking it through has already been done – whereby the author skillfully entertained the reader by the dream children of his fancy.

In the variety of entertainments of this age, – radio, television – theatres etc. the need for activation of brain energies have been sacrificed, through which Self-thought has been neglected. Slowly, ever so slowly, the powerful functions of brain-mind fell into disuse, and begin to atrophy, because entertainment outside of the Small Self is simpler – and less taxing to the subconscious mind. But – the Holy Places of the Gods within you are available – when you have burned through the formidable fortress and ignited the first candle to the union with All-Mind.

If the Pot of Gold at the end of the Rainbow is the goal – then your concentration must be focused on the Ray leading to It, and not upon superficial distractions of the lesser lights, or mortal attractions which lead you away from that gold! Scattered thoughts return scattered dividends, – the interest rate in the Mental Bank, and Credit Card of the Seeker decreases through dissipation of God's majestic mental power within you.

We shall begin our experiment with a simple form of concentration. We realize the difficulties encountered by the average individual when they are directed to concentrate upon an intangibility. It is always simpler to centralize the attention on a visible object or thing.

With this thought in mind, we recommend that you obtain a large sheet of white paper – several feet square. On it, in large letters, you will print ONE THOUGHT. If you prefer to ask a question, use as few words as possible – well defined and complete. Do not become involved in complex situations or questions in the beginning. Thoughts such as: "What causes my headaches? – Is the car safe for our trip? – how long shall I concentrate each day – is another period of the day better for this purpose?" are examples. This form of questioning is for your concentration period. The meditative form follows another pattern, which will be discussed in the Second Discourse. Fasten the sheet of paper at comfortable eye level, to the wall before you, on which you have written your thought. The words should be legible from a distance of five to ten feet. Remove any shiny objects or other distractions from the wall on which you have fastened your paper. The Silence Chamber should not be too warm – as it will induce drowsiness, and a temperature of 68 to 70 degrees is recommended. During Concentration the sense faculties should be keen and alert. Simple deep breathing exercises will be beneficial. We do NOT recommend candles or incense in the early stages of concentration – as the purpose will be defeated if your attention wanders to these external attractions.

Be seated in a comfortable chair, in a relaxed and EXPECTANT frame of mind, hands and legs uncrossed, palms down. A small notebook and pencil on your lap is a necessity at this point, in order that you can write any impression which you receive. Do NOT fail to write whatever you have experienced, or received through mental impressions during this period. Date each entry, and the hour of your concentration. In this manner you will discover that the hour you have chosen is not as successful for you, as the "mood" pattern of individuals will vary. As you continue your concentration practices – the notations in your book will give tangible proof to you at a later time of definite progression. These verifications will be encouraging, and a great boost to your morale.

When you begin this practice of concentration – we recommend that you ALLOW your thoughts to wander! Do not strain in the endeavor to quiet all the thoughts which flow through – but relax – as though you were a bystander, listening to the parade of conversation as it moves through your consciousness. Imagine yourself as a spectator at a parade – your scattered thoughts as the Marchers in the line – and follow them as they pass from the scene. Be detached – as though you were listening to the conversation of another in which you had no personal interest!

In your initial attempts, it might take an hour before this mental conversation and idle wool-gathering ceases. However – if you persevere this method will bring you to a startling conclusion

– "My – there doesn't seem to be very much to think about now. I believe I am ready to concentrate!" You are familiar with the situation of two friends who have met after a separation of many years. At their reunion they are certain that their conversation will flow like a river for many weeks, in an attempt to fill in all events which have transpired since their separation. After a time, there is a lull in their verbal activities – and to their amazement they discover that they are "all talked out."

This is precisely the same process we suggest for the successful termination of wandering thought. We do NOT request our students to "make your mind blank" as this is almost an impossibility in the beginning. The mental world of mind and man, is Eternal – and the Ever-living stream of thought – vibration is continuous. Our goal is to delete the "many thoughts" for the "one." When you have sat quietly for a half hour or longer, and "thought yourself out" – you have arrived at the point of realization that the distractions have been removed and you are free to proceed.

The law which governs this state of being, is a material one. The process of "thinking about everything" has depleted some of the vital energy on the physical plane level, – of your brain mind energies. You are tired mentally – and have exhausted your field of thought. You have come to the place, where you have no desire to "to think about those things" anymore. This is the time for your REAL concentration period, as the Steam Engine of your rambling thought has lost some of its power over you. The Captain, who is ready with the new menu for the day, is able at this point to act as Helmsman of the Good Ship Concentration. When you have reached this point, you will be ready to direct your mental power to the sheet of paper with its question.

READ THE THOUGHT OR QUESTION VERBALLY! Spell it letter by letter – slowly and carefully! THIS IS IMPORTANT! The reason for this procedure shall be enlarged upon in later discourses. This lesson and exercise must remain simple. There is a psychological effect in the verbal repetition of your thought, as it creates a mental assurance that YOU are speaking it! It is being heard! – and your EXPECTANT mood <u>assures</u> you of an answer! Therefore – – since YOU verbally professed the thought or question, you have no further need to consider it – merely to wait for an answer!

When this detail has been attended to – repeat a heartfelt prayer – sing, recite a poem – or prepare yourself in any manner which appeals to the natural instincts of your Ego. Then – VERY casually – direct the attention to the paper on the wall before you. Read it slowly – spelling each letter carefully in your mind. The purpose is to IMPRESS the subconscious that THIS thought – and NONE OTHER – is the focal point of your attention. Each time another thought interferes repeat the procedure from the beginning! The verbal approach is always the most effective. It gives POWER to the thought – that positive power of Impression! It accentuates the sound vibrations in your aura – increasing their vibrational rate.

The whispered words – or mental repetition of the thought are the negative approaches to Concentration! Have you ever seen a lecturer hold his audience spellbound by timidity – feeble or whispered speech? If YOU are not certain of your words or insecure in your question, this same insecurity will be manifested by the timidity in which you gave it expression! Therefore – in your positive declarations – your distinct pronunciation of each letter of your thought, you have mentally reassured yourself. You must convince yourself of the power of your mind and belief in yourself!

The period of Divine Whisperings has not yet arrived. This shall be another development after you have hurdled the first step on the Stairway.

BE verbal! – strong! – positive! – assured!
Whereby you will impress the subconscious with
Confidence that through the will of your conscious
Mind that YOU SHALL SUCCEED!!

Read the words of your thought on the paper, once more. Then dismiss it from your mind. Close your eyes, – and within your mental mirror you will see the after – image of the letters as you have written them. Relax in the pleasant thought that each letter was fashioned by the Fingers of your Mind, – and written on the Wall of the Subconscious. The Message has been delivered! There is nothing left to do but wait for your reply. Each time you refer to the thought again, it "calls it back" and no answer can be received. Be peaceful and content and KNOW that your answer will come. Suddenly a thought will flash through your mind. At the moment it might seem to have no relationship to your question, however, without opening your eyes write the thought you have received in your notebook. (This is easily accomplished with closed eyes if you use the finger of your left hand as a line guide). Continue with your concentration, and as other thoughts enter into your consciousness write them again – and again – and again. If they seem to be unrelated and entirely irrelevant to your question and inconsequential, open your eyes and start over. PATIENCE! PERSEVERANCE! Remember the sixteenth letter!

For an analogy we will assume you had asked a question about treatments for a physical discomfort, and needed advice whether or not to continue this therapy. Perhaps "Yes" was your first response – followed by a "no." This would be confusing to the beginner – yet the method MUST be continued, as in time to come, you will be at the point where you will recognize that the instantaneous response from the Intuitive Self is always the correct answer. After a period of time has elapsed you will learn to discard the second, third or fourth answers. You must BELIEVE in the responses from your own Soul Ego – through which the highest Minds may transmit their thought impulses. During your first weeks of experimentation with this exercise the thoughts will often be questioning ones. i.e. "I wonder if I made this up – I think I will ask again – No, that couldn't have been right – I wonder – oh, oh, now I have another answer – which one is right?" etc. etc. This type of mental conversation must be discarded, and it will cease after a time. It is a form of mental negation which is traditional with all seekers and eventually as the rapport condition between Conscious and Diviner Subconscious is established it ceases entirely.

REMEMBER!! – NO ONE is infallible! You will err many times in your interpretations of the thought received. However, if you are faithful in your experimentations, and continue writing your impressions, the undeniable proof of increasing accuracy will overwhelm you. As the HABIT of concentration continues the HABIT of response will become the HABIT of the subconscious mind. This harmonious co-operation of the Law and HABIT of conscious and subconscious self, is the basic foundation for the evolution of the Ego.

It is a joyful adventure across the threshold to the boundless Ocean of Infinity. When you – as Conqueror – have subdued the wandering sheep of your mind, you will stand firmly and proudly on that first step, as a lamb at the feet of the Shepherd.

Although the Seeker might be an intellectual giant with an intelligence quotient of highest degree – no spiritual vistas or Cosmic consciousness can fill the Cup – until the formidable foe of wandering thought is conquered. The second step of Meditation will lead you to the Starlight, on the fringe of Infinity. This Eternal Ocean of unlimited depth lies within yourself, the Cosmic Bowl of spiritual rejuvenation. In a third form, Contemplation leads you through the sacred veil – the Eye of the Shining Star.

Meditation – Divine Whisperings

The Conqueror – proud of his successful
Journey, stands at the Threshold, happy
In the reward of the First Star which
he holds in his hand.

We shall review our understanding of Concentration versus Meditation! "Concentration is the act of focusing the attention, through mental powers of mind, on ONE subject – object or thing. It is the outer manifestation, or it's objective form."

Meditation, is the utilization of this same concentration, directed towards Realization of God, and becoming one with Him, – within the Self. Meditation is that same concentration directed INWARDS, to subjectivity, or the inner nature of Self – Being – or God.

Since you, as Conqueror have advanced to the plane of sustained concentration and one-pointedness you have qualified for admittance to that Inner Palace, – the Divine State of Being. This is a higher dimension of the Self, where you will touch the hem of His Garment, through communion with your own Soul – e.g. – Christ-of-God-within.

The vague thoughts, distractions, or attention directed to various outer attractions are the factors which have deterred you from establishing a communion with the Soft Small Voice within, – before you became the new Conqueror. You were beset with mental queries of "why?" – how? – who? – which? – yes – no – what for? – and why not?" – a babbling of tongue so distressing to your peace of mind. But now – as the Conqueror you can be proud of the power YOU have over these "evils" which had tempted you. You are ready and eager to sit at the feet of your master, in spiritual meditation, and are proud of your spiritual maturity, which you have earned through your own efforts. You are able to sit passively now and listen to the lesson of the day.

In a normal span of life, the small child approaches his father in complete confidence with minor problems which upset him. His manner is direct and to the point, as is the nature of a child. "Father I have a problem which I can't understand. Will you help me – can you answer it?" He is definite and assured that his father will assist him. His parent smiles, "Yes child, if you will be quiet and listen, I will try to give you the answer."

Approach to God, through Meditation
Is as simple as that!)

Therefore – as this natural condition exists in your objective world, then the law which governs it, must likewise function in the spiritual. How much greater is the wisdom of the unlimited Infinite word – or the Mind of the Heavenly Father!!

The World of Form contains many fallacies and half-truths, which reveal themselves through their sense perceptions to the consciousness. Since there are malfunctions of these sense organs, their transmission to the conscious mind are not entirely reliable. The unadulterated truth in its pristine purity is not possible through the objective plane of limited consciousness. But the unobstructed Infinite Universe can reveal the Truth – or the answer to every need. All is known through Infinite Reflection. The reply is THERE – before you have spoken! GOD HAS HEARD! HE IS THERE! HE ALWAYS ANSWERS! – if you listen!

But alas, as our Little Joe discovered, it was necessary to travel the highways and byways before the wandering sheep of his mind, with their false concepts could be uprooted and planted anew.

Countless complex theories have been expounded – and difficult assignments given to the student in ancient and newer schools of thought. This has handicapped the average "Little Joe" – and filled him with discouragement through his inability to fulfill these tasks. Mortal mind led him far afield during his search – away from the very God of his own Being whom he sought, and could not find within himself!

The Initiate since ancient times was required to pass through trials, penances, sacrifices, rituals, exercises, etc. – and other acts of OUTER demonstrations to punish the body into submission. It was believed that the outer form was a necessity to establish communion with Him.

If you have sincerely considered the dual faculty of your being, (mind and soul), – with its objectivity in concentration – then you can realize that its subjective state in meditation, is the passive and inner faculty. The processes to reach this Inner world within yourself, should not be complex – only mental control. Each disorganized thought thrown out into the Sea of Thought adds to the multiplicity of thought – clusters of the world, until the Highway of this stream is dense with the cross current of negative thought-vibrations. Their power increased through cohesion – revealing themselves as mental thought forms – or undirected "entities" in the world in which you live. Our discourse on Thought and Its Form will be discussed in another Series.

The quiet unruffled pool of mind – with its serenity and true reflections, is the treasure at the end of your rainbow! Within this clear pool you will find no distortions – or fuzzy and blurred reflections. Clear perception of the Light of Christ mind shall be yours – as He can only be a reflection in a mirror-like calm! The shining goal of the Conqueror is the holy privilege of having union with the true Image, and the reflection within himself. In your union with the master, error is impossible, – as error owes its existence only through comparison. With the Master, as THE mind of your body – there can be NO comparison for he IS the Light of your World – that mental light which leads to Cosmic Consciousness.

There have been several repetitions during our discourses regarding the line of distinction between the phases of concentration and meditation.

Our purpose is to impress this distinction indelibly in your consciousness. The definitive line is self evident in the nature of the two words. OBJECTIVE – (concentration) as object – or outer: Subjective (meditation), as "sub" or below – and inner. Objective form is that of the world of limitation – principally that with which you are normally conversant. Subjectivity is the realm just below the surface, or a realm into which you must retreat, and "retire" from the objects in the line of vision. In the objective form your awareness is third dimensional – length, depth and breadth. When you enter into the deeper state (subjectivity) you add another dimension, – the inner form of consciousness. In the first aspect (concentration) the powers of mind are direction of will – or the positive directiveness of mental energies. In the meditative phase the reverse is encountered. The negative (or passive) condition is a requirement. You are NOT the director of the flow of thought, but the receiver of it, from the infinite mind within yourself. You will graduate from the degree of Observer – to that of the Knower.

Your entry on this step of the journey to the rainbow is the second step, where you shall explore the field of consciousness on a deeper level – through the fourth dimensional stage of consciousness. This fourth dimensional state of being is not a physical property, – but one of ethereal and Cosmic nature, as another extension of yourself. If consciousness in its second form (subconscious), were not available to you – there would be no possibility for an "extension" of the consciousness into Time-Space relativity. The Conscious

Mind is held to its own limitations of the three D's (length, depth and breadth), – and the existence of the mortal without the addition of the Holy Fourth, would be dreary indeed. If you were held to the limitations of the five faulty senses, divine self could not leave it a tomb. It would be a pitiful existence for the self-conscious entity, living in a form, devoid of imagination – creativeness – or responsibility to Higher Minds. A beggared – sad – Self!

REMEMBER:

Concentration – the objective form (objects) third dimension

Meditation – the subjective (inner) 4th dimension

Deeper meditation can extend itself beyond the fourth dimension – but of this we shall speak about in later instructions.

The First Heaven can be gained through meditation – the second and third heavens in the deeper stages – but NONE can be reached until the Ogre of Concentration has been conquered!!

Our approach to meditation shall control another facet of this wondrous mind power. For our study, we shall assume that you have persevered with the first lesson, and are ready for the second step. Since the goal is the knowledge of Self – all that which the Ego, through its many lives acquired, meditation shall lead you into the realm of Soul – and the Whispers from the Master Self. Therefore, the preparations for the meditative period are altered to coincide with the holiness of this Great Adventure.

Little Joe is ready – he has matured!

Meditation – The Procedure

The room which you have chosen for your Silence Chamber should be well ventilated, comfortably warm, but never beyond 72 degrees. A lethargic state, without falling into a deep sleep is to be desired; comfortable clothing, relaxed, joyful state of mind is a requisite.

REMEMBER: – You are entering into an adventure in which you shall eventually meet the Master – become the Knower, – and see His Image within yourself! This is the most exciting experience of your life, and the ultimate height of Cosmic consciousness is predicated by your own perseverance and application. All the intellectual or academic knowledge which you have acquired in a life time of living, can NOT produce this state of Cosmic consciousness – but only give you the classification of an intelligent ego. This classification can apply to anyone who can read applies himself studiously in the field of academic training. Meditation in its holiest form brings forth the Mind of Christ – to the forefront of Conscious Self. When mortal consciousness is overshadowed by its Cosmic state, no title or University degree can compete with the Degree of Spiritual Rejuvenation. This transcendental state is earned through the teardrops of love – holy devotion and ceaseless effort!

Prepare a simple altar for your Silence Chamber – a vase of flowers, picture, candles and incense. The psychological effect created by the outer symbols will be uplifting to your consciousness. Before you are seated light the candles and incense, and relax in a comfortable position. A brief prayer should preface this meditation period. The rhythmic breath presented with this lesson will assist you in becoming passive. You are not to confuse this type of breath with the physical culture exercise, as our purpose is not to achieve a tonic effect within the body, or activation of the senses. The reverse condition of passivity is desired for meditation.

During normal consciousness the five sense faculties bombard the brain mind with the impulses and messages received through these organs of sense. Our exercise will subdue the outer senses (of conscious mind), – and assist you in entering the subjective state of passivity. The simile of shedding the clothing of your work day – in exchange for the slumber – garment of the night, reflects the desired state of consciousness in meditation.

The ancient Hindus compared the subjective manner of breathing to a fine silken cord – silvery in appearance, which is drawn up through the body, then exhaled. This is the thread of consciousness between the two worlds – and dimensions beyond. As you breathe, retain the thought that each inhalation or exhalation is in harmony with Universal Breath – out of the Breath of God, the universal essence of your Being. The harmony and rhythm of the Universe is eternal and steadfast in its three phases of pulsation and motion.

The simple analogy of the ocean waves with their white caps, would exemplify this point, of the triune pulsation. The wave rises to the count of one, holds it at a crest for count two – then descends to its third point, continuing in this rhythmic pattern of Eternal motion. This is everlasting – the majestic cosmic rhythm. The Power of the breath in you contains the Secret Key to His Mansion!

The Eternal Vibration is constant (motion), – and Universal in its action and after effect – likewise the rhythm, and harmony of mortal exists in the same pattern in his finite world. Your world – as part of the Macrocosm MUST be in harmony with the universal motion. The outer world (objective) reacts to outer impulses – the Inner World (subjective) reflects its impulses to the Outer You! Therefore, harmony must be brought about between the two aspects of yourself. Three points of your triune being, shall produce this result! Mind – Breath – Consciousness – are the trinity of your meditation. "I think – I breathe – I AM!

The pulsations of the Greater Universe affect the outer and inner self. Your life pulsations depend upon the Cosmic breath and rhythm. Your union with Him – through It – depend on YOU!! You can never know Him in fullness, unless your microcosmic world is in sympathetic harmony with the macrocosm.

The rhythmic breath is very effacious during any time of stress – concern or anger. It will restore balance in the body more rapidly than harmful barbiturates. It has a sedative effect on the nervous system, and the action of the body. If you suffer from insomnia, this rhythmic breath will assist you if you practice it at bedtime. When your consciousness is centered in this, it cannot be engaged in other distracting thoughts!

Rhythmic Breath – The Stabilizer

Place the forefinger of your right hand on the left pulse. Note the pulsation and accustom yourself to the rhythmic beat of its action. Count the pulsation in their cadence of rise and fall – with the count of one to six: i.e. o n e --- t w o – t h r e e – f o u r, f i v e – s i x. Your six-count rhythm will be distinctive unlike another's, as the fluctuations between rise and fall are individual. Practice this for a period of time, until you have established a mental coordination with the cadence, and have memorized the rise and fall, in your verbal count. When you have established the rhythm you can discontinue the verbal repetition.

As you continue the practice of rhythmic breathing, you will decrease the rush of blood to the brain and quiet the activity of thought-impulses. The decreased pulsations are beneficial to the preparatory step of meditation. When you have familiarized yourself with your pulse rhythm, sit in a comfortable chair hands and feet uncrossed, eyes closed, – and inhale to the count of six. (Remember – YOUR pulse rhythm. Visualize within yourself a spider like silken thread of breath rising though the centre of your body localizing itself in the centre of your head. Hold the breath to the count of six – then exhale though the nostrils to the same rhythmic six-count. The three steps of breath should be consistent, the exhalations in same ratio as the inhalations. Repeat this exercise three times, – during the first month of experimentation. As you become more proficient in the spiritual breath, you can increase it to seven times before each meditation.

If you have never practiced the six-count breath, you might experience a light headed feeling, or slight dizziness. Do not be alarmed, as this is a natural condition – due to your inexperience with the method. Under the personal supervision of a Master, the rhythmic breath can be deepened to experience the higher form of Samadhi. We cannot divulge this form of breath in a public place, – unless you are under personal observation.

The Jet Age in which you live is geared towards speed – it is a tempo predicated by the urge to "possess – advance – do things – and go places." This accelerated pace is out of harmony with the peaceful cosmic rhythm, and creates imbalance in the material and psychic selves. The human heart, the Ruler of precious life blood, is taxed beyond endurance to supply its human Temple in the violent agitation to live twice the life span, in one half the time.

The owner of the bodily temple gives little thought to the precious heart – the pulse beat of his private universe, which beats constantly without rest – to take care of bodily needs. He urges it onward – for more production faster – faster – faster – until the ruling King, loyal to the body it is glorifying, is exhausted from the pace, and withdraws from earthly competition!

Beloved Ones – cease your speed, and come into the peaceful calm of Universal Rhythm. Breathe quietly and calmly – in order that the ruler of your temple can curtail his labor and extend the life expectancy of his framework, and increase your peace of mind. His role of beating in harmony with the universal rhythmic pulse, cannot be accomplished without the cooperation of the mortal whom he serves and quickens. Your efforts towards rhythmic breath, and mental control will produce dual results – in the effects on the inner and outer man, through whom the egoic personality is reflected! Your state of wellbeing – peaceful attitude – and rejuvenation of the bodily functions, will be magnified in your vibrant harmonious vibrations.

Your Concentration period was of an objective or material nature. As you enter the meditative state, the subjective or inner and spiritual thought should be held in mind. If you have been persistent in your initial efforts, your need of the white sheet of paper, as a focal point, has ceased. You should be able at this point to enter into the subtler state of subjectivity with ease. NOW is the time for Divine Whisperings. During Concentration your efforts were vocal – in meditation the reverse is true, they are soft whispered commands or requests of the Inner Self.

With quiet voice, whisper a spiritual question or thought, as though you were offering it to the Inner Self in secret confession. Explain to your "self" that this is your period of sharing, – and your desire to be a bosom companion with the master self. After you have whispered your thought or request, release it – and listen to the words which "move through your mind." In your experimental stages with this form of meditation, – do not write in your notebook. (It might distract you from the subjective state). Your entries should be made after you have completed your meditation.

REMEMBER: – In the serene and placid state of mind, your consciousness is intensified – and the psychic senses with their vibrational thought – impulses are keen. Instead of the harsher sounds of the physical world, and ceaseless clamor, the sound waves of higher frequencies of the inner world, will be soft and muted. The sensory perceptions will seem to be coming from a great distance. You will "hear within your mind" as though you were coming out from under an anesthetic – and the inner interpretations of symbols and form will be hazy and fleeting. In your relaxed hypnogogic state, you will be able to differentiate between the harsh sounds of the physical dimension and those of the finer inner world. The "whisperings" will move through mind like a silken thread. Often with one word a sentence or complete thought will be realized.

REMEMBER: You are seeking the key of communion with Him within yourself. You want to share, – and because of the duality of all nature and things, it is impossible to do so – without a Mind to share with!! Therefore, in meditation you will learn to listen to that which the master shares with you. Beloved One, do not whisper in a continual flow of words – without waiting for his reply! Then – when He has replied, acknowledge the message, – and continue your whispered conversation.

A simulated conversation of a student at meditation is given, to assist you in understanding this method. YOU – the Conscious Self will begin the conversation. He – the Inner master – will reply.

You: I must learn how to do this – where shall I begin? I have been told to whisper my questions, but I don't know what to ask.

(STOP RIGHT THERE and listen to the thought moving through your mind).

He: Yes – you have many questions, we know.

You: That startled me! It was just as though I answered myself.

He: You did indeed. You knew the words you would say before they were spoken.

You: I did? I don't see how that could be. I just thought of them and said them.

He: But dear Child, where did the thought come from which you spoke?

You: It came from myself

He: Are you certain?

You: Well, I thought I was, but now I have to think about it.

He: Ah, – at last – we have established communication, – you have begun to question. When you ask, an answer MUST be forthcoming, etc. etc.

Beloved One – the words we have given are only an outline – as an example of conversation with Him. It will not follow this pattern with each ego, as it is personalization of the Inner Self. It manifests the attributes in myriad form, and unpredictable manner. This Meditative "idea" is only a key with which you can unlock the inner door to the kingdom.

REMEMBER: You can RECEIVE nothing – if your whisper is continuous. You MUST wait for the reply. You are NOT on a party line, with all keys open on your switchboard. Your Meditation Dial is marked, "Private Line to the Master." YOU dial the number, as you hold the receiver, and wait for him to answer. When he replies – you receive – and acknowledge his answer. Your circuit is the telephone line, with its negative and positive current. The flow of thought is through the route of Consciousness which travels over the circuit, entering conscious mind as a thought vibration. You understand the thought, and re-translate it in your own words!!

Later, in the deeper forms of meditation you will be able to enter into the joy of long distance conversation – but at this point, your "whisperings" are from the frequency level of the subjective plane. The Master-mind (Cosmic) frequency is a telephone connection of subtler degree. This second step of endeavor is reception on the Intuitive level, – through your own subjectivity. YOU are the Seeker who inquires – and the master self replies.

A meditation period should be of 30 to 60 minutes duration. The regularity of your daily devotion WILL bring results. Through your consecrated Whisperings, you will unite with the Diviner Cosmic-Master-link.

May your initial Whispers lead you into the awesome splendour of the Silence before His Cosmic Cathedral, where His mind will be your mind, and his celestial song of Love, the joy of your heart!

Contemplation – The Disciplinarian

"Seek ye first the Kingdom of Heaven, and all shall be added unto you."

You have travelled quite a distance since your first faltering Step on the Path. The Ogre has been conquered – and the Star was your reward. Your second step prepared you for subjugation of conscious self, – and carried you through the doorway into the Inner World. Your faint whisperings are more confident and now you are able to respond to the higher frequencies which will greet you at this third point. The second star which you received for your endeavors will shed its light in the second chamber of your realization. The third – and crucial point – of your initiation into His upper Kingdom, is the path of the patient disciple. This is the Disciplinary Road which many begin – but only a handful complete the goal. The first two steps will fade into nothingness

– when they are compared with the Master – Contemplation. He beckons – let us move swiftly towards him, before we weaken.

The Third Step: Contemplation – The Disciplinarian

"Many are called – but few are chosen"

In the words of the great Webster, the contemplator is "one who contemplates – with intent." We take the liberty of adding to this definition "one who contemplates – towards the fulfillment and purpose of his vision." When you approach the third Step of the Way, you have advanced beyond the phase of Inquirer – or Receiver – and are on the Threshold of becoming: THE THINKER!

Concentration, or meditation would serve no utilitarian purpose, if the evolving Ego had no goal, aim or desire for ultimate success. If you have reached the third point of your Path, with hunger in your heart to KNOW you are victor over the first two, and have earned the reward of Contemplation.

If our words have been read in a superficial manner – without application, then this third step will hold no charm for you. This Golden Star is treasured by the humble disciple who comes to His feet to worship. It is the disciplinary path for which you have been prepared. Its rewards will be according to your perseverance.

You will recall – from our concentration discourse with its initiatory form of discipline, that the first approach on the Path was the verbal, or outer form. The second Step led you into the inner state of whispered communion (subjectivity). The Contemplative Step is your role as The Thinker – thinking from within yourself, in sequential fashion, – and arriving at a summation of the thought, before the Silent period is over.

During your period of contemplation you will discipline yourself to think "beyond" the thought – trace it to its origin, – and derive from it the ultimate of its essence. You will convey the series of impressions from the inner recesses to the outer mind. To assist you in understanding the procedure, we will use a tangible objective with which you are familiar. A piano – as a musical instrument will be the focal point of our example.

First: We will catalogue the piano in the qualifications of a Concentrator. At that point you would see the objective details of the instrument – admire its beauty, grace, and perhaps recollect familiar melodies or unusual tonal qualities. You would analyze the melodies, – which in turn, would bring to mind some circumstances connected with them.

Step Two: In your subjective state (as meditator) your meditations would lead to observations of the instrument from the subjective standpoint. You would feel the inner nature of the instrument – or travel with the sound vibrations of its keyboard. You would respond to the cosmic hum of its lingering melodies. The subjective senses would be stimulated by the remembered vibrations, which in turn would re-unite you with familiar scenes, incidences or situations in which the piano was the key note. In the deeper stages of meditation, you would mentally move "from" the piano – to the personality who played the music, – and receive information about the pianist. In the subjective state your five senses would function on their own plane.: i.e.: feeling the excellent quality of its grain, and satiny finish, – hearing the sound vibrations, – seeing a scene through mental reflection – and perhaps utilizing the sense of smell to recognize flowers near the instrument. The five sense faculties would be involved to a greater or lesser degree.

The Third Step – as Contemplator:

You have completed the outer and inner observations (of step one and two) which were more or less rudimentary. But now – as the Thinker – the instrument is ready to reveal more to you. You are prepared to THINK!

You ask of the inner self: "What is the piano made of – ? the wood is beautiful." Mentally – in succeeding stages, your consciousness extends itself to trace the wood to the mill where it was pressed, cut and assembled in preparation for its musical life. But as a Thinker, you are not satisfied with this meager information. You KNOW there is much more to be made known to you about the wood. "What forest – what land – what area – what country – did this beautiful wood come from?" Your consciousness extends through thought projection to the forest where the trees grew – of such rare lumber. Ah – but as the Thinker your survey is still incomplete. Your eagerness will carry your further. "I have seen the forest – now I must KNOW the cycle in which these trees were planted. – – Who placed the seeds in the ground? Were they tenderly planted as we cover our seedlings – or did the forest grow from seeds, which were carried by birds? – or – were they hidden by squirrels for their winter food and forgotten?" As a Disciplinarian you have conquered your wandering thought, and will NOT be tempted to follow the squirrels – or the birds in flight. You will NOT be sidetracked from your objective – and will hold the contemplative thought until you arrive at the cycle or time, in which the forest was born!

When you have completed this portion of the survey, and are unable to go beyond that – the accumulated information will be a rewarding revelation. This is the method that the disciplined Thinker would follow.

You return from your mental reflections, with the desire to know how the keyboard was fashioned – why each string, chord or paddle was united in a distinctive fashion. Your contemplation will relay the information to your mind, of the relationship between the piano, harpsichord, clavichord, virginal, etc. – and propel you into the Time Space cycle in which instrumental music was first introduced. In your disciplinary path you will NOT deviate from the original trend of thought – or follow sidelines of the first objective – but will continue until you reach the Cause! The effects you are aware of (the piano) – as it was the original object of your Contemplation.

Beloved Ones – this is Master – contemplation!

Many thoughts will be laid on the Table of your Lord during this third step. If you are a sincere disciple, you will pursue the thought until you have arrived at the Cause. If you have no tangible objective in mind (i.e. as a piano), – and your thought for contemplation is of a personal or impersonal nature, the method of arriving at the Cause would be the same.

Little Joe, – as our Thinker – will assist us in exemplifying this form of contemplation.

We will assume that he has been unhappy about the strained situation existing between himself and his good friend John. It is not necessary for Little Joe to concentrate for an objective solution – nor to receive a subjective answer to his problem. He is deeply concerned over personal differences which have arisen in their relationship with each other. He COULD ask for a solution of this situation (through concentration), – but even this would not be the answer to his problem. If he meditated on the subject – and a solution was given through this form, – it might not satisfy him completely – if it did not DISSOLVE the problem. A "surface" solution would only be the aspirin which anaesthetized the headache – but did not reveal its Cause!

Therefore, Little Joe MUST resort to the contemplative method – in which he will trace the beginning of their difficulties – back to the Cause. Little Joe would proceed with the self-examination in a reverent manner; he would NOT allow himself to be swayed by personal opinions – or become side tracked into pleasanter fields. He would be honest in his declarations – and wait for the reply.

We will eavesdrop on Little Joe, as he prepares himself for the third step.

"Dear God – John and I have been friends for many years. I don't want to lose his friendship – but there is something in our relationship these past months which is annoying to both of us. I am upset every time I see him, and dread the club meetings that I must attend with him. I can't avoid them either. What is wrong

– why do we both feel this way?" (Have you been aware that Little Joe no longer asks 'what shall I do? – Ah! He has progressed!)

Little Joe waits patiently – assured that all will be explained to him. A thought moves through his mind, – and suddenly he sees the mental image of John, with a pained expression. "That's odd, I can't remember him looking like that." (ah, but yes you can Joe. Remember when John was elected club treasurer and you twitted him publicly about running off with the money?) "Oh – that was nothing, I was only joking with him." (Joe, are you sure? Wasn't there a hidden barb in your remark?") But of course not! I know he's not a thief! Why – he's my best friend). (Joe – Joe – THINK! You know there is more to your feeling than that, don't soft-soap your conscience like that. Come on Joe, THINK!) "I'm thinking, but I can't see anything important in my remarks to him, – it was such a little thing." (No, Little Joe, admit to yourself, that you did resent John's election as treasurer. You wanted the office yourself.) "That's not true – he is more qualified than I am." (Ah ha! Now we are getting someplace Joe. You DO have resentment which you haven't admitted to yourself). "Well, all right, I'll admit to a little resentment, but I got over that." (Did you now? – are you sure you aren't holding a grudge?). "Well, if I am no one knows about it." (Oh yes, they do – you might pat John on the back and tell him he's doing a good job, but your thoughts are not as sincere as you profess. John feels it). "Oh my gosh, do you suppose he knows?" (yes, he does, Joe, he knows something is wrong, he senses it. Remember your resentment is on a low frequency on the negative plane, – it is not the same frequency you had shared with him before. John recognizes the difference. He is very puzzled Joe, and you better square yourself with him.) "You mean I have to TELL him?" (yes, talk it over with him, and put your cards on the table, he will respect you for it – wish him well and MEAN it. It won't do much good if you just say the words, you must MEAN it – and it must be cleared with the Big Man in you, Joe. "Well I'll be dog goned, I would never have thought such a little thing – as my remark – his feelings, and my hidden resentment would create so much friction, I'll do it, – thank you for the help." (Wait a minute – we're not finished). "What?" – I thought this was all there was to Contemplation. All we did was analyze the situation and reason about it, – now that I've got the answer, isn't that enough?" (NO, not nearly enough. Come back here and sit down). "Okay, so that happens now?" (Joe – THINK! Remember you are a Thinker now, so get busy and do so!) Pause – and more pauses. "All right, so I'm thinking, and nothing happens. What am I supposed to be thinking about?" (your resentment Little Joe – your resentment. Why did you resent John? Why did you feel you could have handled the job better? – why did you twit him about 'walking off with the treasury' – think Joe – think!) pause – pause (ah, we see a picture is beginning to form in your mind). "Oh – my – you mean my resentment goes back that far, to the year I held the Treasurer's office in college and messed up the books and lost my job?" (yes, Joe, but go back farther than that. That's not all of it – carry on) "Hummm – there's another picture coming to my mind. I think I was about 14, a scrawny kid too working for a prize in a magazine seeing contest. My buddy and I wanted to take the trip together which they offered us. Our votes were pretty close, – it looked like we would get to earn the prize. It seems to me he reminded me of John too." (you're beginning to get the picture now Joe). "Yes, – I guess so – oh I don't like this one of myself. I remember now – – I thought I had the prize cinched so I didn't bother selling more magazines. Hank continued and he and another kid won the trip – while I loafed on the job. I remember I was very angry and we got into a big fight. I thought he was sneaky and that it was his move to let me know we were getting close to my record. I never did make up with him either." (yes Joe, you have done well, can you see now how far back your resentment is traced? It has always been against the "other fellow" – when the cause was within yourself. Do you understand yourself better now Joe? It has taken you a long time to get to the Cause, but you have been creating effects with it all though your life. Come on Joe, how about clearing up the records with John?) "I will – I will".

Beloved Ones, THIS is the contemplation of a Thinker. Perhaps you will say, "but that is only thinking, reasoning and analyzing," as Joe said but we repeat that it is MORE than this, since Master-contemplation traces the objective form (or thought), to its source, and derives every iota of realization out of the original form. Although we have given two illustrations on the material plane level, using objects or personal examples, the method involved in reaching the Cause on the Diviner planes is pursued in the same manner.

Let us assume – in your endeavour to KNOW YOURSELF – or the manner in which you were created, – that you sat with this intention for the subject of your contemplation. Although the admonition has been shouted from rooftops since time immemorial – MAN, KNOW THYSELF! Only the minority heed the words, or strive to reach the Truth of their own being. Our third illustration will bring out points to consider, from the vantage point of a Thinker.

"God – what am I? – Mind – Body – Soul – Ego – Consciousness? – am I more than one? Am I dual – if so, why am I dual? – I am triune also – but WHY? Since I am composed of so many things, elements, principles, gasses, minerals, chemicals, and I exist, then in some manner I must have come into Being? HOW? – What is my relationship to the Source? What is the Source? How does it enter into this "thing" which I call myself? Dear Ones, this form of questioning is brief. If you spent an entire lifetime in the study of YOUR relationship to the Universal Soul (within yourself and your fellow creatures) you would never reach the point of satiation. Therefore, we will follow Little Joe as he pursues this subject from a Diviner plane.

It is simpler – in the first experiments with Divine Contemplation to begin with the mortal body, – that something of which you have conscious knowledge. Little Joe enters into this form of contemplation with a desire to know something of the mechanics of his body – the wondrous manner in which muscles move and bend, – and cooperate with him in his embodied cycle. He looks within himself to find the reason for their functioning in response to his verbal command, or the involuntary motions which are controlled by the subconscious functions. The astonishing fact of the involuntary actions, which he does not command in each second of his existence, – their coordination and functions startle him with the wonder of this creation – himself! He would contemplate the "how" of their actions, – he would question "why." He would learn of the association between conscious and subconscious selves. He would take this thought further – into the relationship with the super conscious, and its affiliation with the dual portions of himself. Revelation upon revelation would be unfolded for him, as he delved more deeply into the activities of himself as a created being – that Living Soul!

He would feel an upsurge of pride, that he, like all other conscious entities was the vehicle for the Soul – wherein his egoic personality could express itself through that Divine Temple. His contemplation would lead him further – to the energies which caused the body to function – and that wondrous discovery within himself, that anything which had action – must have a POWER behind it to bring about the action.

He would gasp in amazement that he had not thought of himself in this manner before, and taken the glory of the body-form as a matter of course! As Little Joe persevered in his study of Man, he would "break down" the particles which entered into the body structure. He would begin with the formation of flesh – tissues, veins – arteries, blood, cells, molecules, form, structure, nature – polarity – vibrations – and the cohesive law which held this Temple in a state of form. Through his deeper search, in this regressive method, he would be led to trace the atoms of his being to their Source. By the time Little Joe had completed a small portion of his survey, of the creature Man, his spiritual and intellectual growth would be astonishing, and a revelation to himself.

If you – through your endeavours, have touched the Hem of Contemplation in this manner, you will not be able to restrain yourself from following the Light. The Cosmic Masters smile on the Thinker – and the wisdom of the ages is available to he "who hath ears to hear with, and eyes to see." If you have the courage, fortitude and intestinal stamina to continue, the doors to the Third Kingdom will open wide for you, If you procrastinate until "sometime when I get around to it," you shall only see that Kingdom through another's eyes, – the eyes of those who HAD the courage, determination, desire and patient qualities through which they were able to reflect the nature of the Master!

"Are ye Ready – Are ye able? Said the Master. Are ye?"

Have you spoken about Cosmic illumination – Cosmic Consciousness – Realization – and "thought" you have experienced it? Ah, Beloved Ones, when you have only "thought" you have experienced this illumination, then it has not yet been thine. When it has been glorified in you – and poured forth from you like a fountain, and quickened your Being with its radiant flame, YOU will KNOW! All who enter your presence will KNOW! The steps to the Eternal Flame, the Living Fire of God in You always expresses itself through the form. KNOW THYSELF! – Dear Ones, – "thyself" is only made known – through thy own self – the Divine in You.

The paths of Concentration, leading TO Meditation – FROM Meditation INTO Contemplation, will bring their own reward, for "he who seeks is sure to find."

Children Beloved: – for countless ages you have searched among the ruins, and the heights. You have walked in many gardens, and travelled in and out of streams in your ceaseless search. The Ego strives eternally to find that "something" – and because of its illusive quality, and its accelerated vibration, it is not easily grasped. But the runner who is fleet of foot and mind, is able to reach the side of his target and remain united with him, when they travel the highways and byways – mind with mind. The haggard remains behind, his goal post always beyond the horizon. When you have joined The Companion on the trail – there is no separation, no urgency, – no necessity for haste. You have met with the Master, and in the serenity of His mind, your spirit is unruffled, serene and blissful. Your queries are instantly answered, – the desired knowledge is immediately available. No arduous hours of preparation will then be necessary, when the earthling Master has met with the Cosmic One, the Beloved of His heart. His knowledge will be your knowledge, – His wisdom will flow through you, for at this point you will have come to know – and understand the esoteric meaning of the Christ's words,

"I and my Father are One!"

Contemplation:
The moments of contemplation are the
Sacred moments when sublime images take
Possession of the consciousness of
The disciple.

Contemplation is indispensable for the
Disciple, for during these moments he
Sets his inner life in order and gains
Control over himself.
(from Sacred Words of the Master,
Belinda Douno)

James 1:5 If any of you lack wisdom, let him ask of God that giveth to all men liberally, and upbraideth not; and it shall be given him.

Samadhi – (Ecstasy) – The King!

(Though I am apart from Thee, I shall be with Thee always).
The Christ

Samadhi is a Sanskrit term, its definition being: 'putting together – profound meditation, absorption in the spirit. The final stage in the practice of Yoga, in which the individual becomes one with the object of meditation, thus attaining a condition of super consciousness and unqualified blissfulness, which is called 'moksha.'

Although the Hindus have defined this condition to a brief paragraph, the attainment of the holy fourth step of Samadhi is very lengthy. It is every Soul-ego's realization and desire to dwell with full consciousness in the Temple of the Living God!

Those who walk this path, remove their sandals, as they follow the footsteps of the masters on sacred soil. The Egoic personality, who has reached this point of evolution, approaches the Altar of the Lord, faces Him in the East, and with faith and passivity of a small child renounces the mortal Will for His! If your probationary path has brought you to the doorway of the King, you have passed beyond the confusion of an undisciplined subconscious self, and are prepared to receive Him. You are ready for the Throne Room in the Mountain of Illumination, and your patient devotion has given you the right to wear the crown of Christ – the King!

The stairway of entry into illumination, Ecstasy, and holy blissful Samadhi is difficult to describe. The defined condition of "putting together" signifying "union" leaves much to the imagination of the reader. However, it is a state of Being – condition of mind – an elevation of consciousness – transcending the mortal limitations of Self-consciousness. Your material boundaries extend into and through the horizon where the shimmering veil of Cosmic vibration and flame of Being beckon. As you move through this portal, you quiver on the brink of Eternity, and glory in the realization of the flame of God Soul within yourself.

The state of Cosmic consciousness, reached through the doorway of Samadhi is one of exquisite light. Its impact is so acutely magnified that seconds pass for eternity, and time space seems to cease. In the supreme moment when the King ascends the Throne of Infinity, you are All – and All is yourself! During this state of suspended animation, the finite world is but a speck on the horizon of your mind. The clarion call of Soul is Ruler Absolute; – the absence of mortal sound is vibrant within you – as thousands of angels with their sweet notes of cosmic love thrill your Being. In the ecstasy of your Illumination no thing is withheld from you – God is One! – You are He! – He is You! Liquid Light fills your being – its flame of warmth and cold thrill you with the bliss of knowing yourself as All. Your joy meets joy – thought greets thought, love feeds love, all is peace. The sunlight, moonlight, firelight, starlight – oceans, rivers, planets, galaxies, – all are yours – and they exist in You, and you exist in them! The compassion of Christ lights your Being with the message: all become your brothers and sisters within the instant – and the realization thrills your Being with the holy revelation of this Infinite relationship. Higher – higher – higher – your racing Ego moves into Light, and with an exhilarating joy you yearn to hold the world in your arms with love. You have become the World – in this moment of union. The true God-Soul is everywhere, at every point within itself, in yourself, and in all things. YOU ARE that Illuminated One, that limitless, expandable I, – all Mind – all Soul – all heart – all love – all Light!

Every element of life, animal, vegetable and mineral are felt within you separately and collectively. The trilling sound of the bird is your sound, the laughter of young lovers is your laughter – the sweetness of a newborn babe is your birth; – you are the proud parent – you are all – that Infinite One!

You KNOW the dim and bright places – the vibrations of the Cosmic message of Infinity flows through you in its movement through cosmic spheres. You question no longer, "who am I – from whence have I come – why – and what have I come to learn?" All is known for YOU have become the Knower. "Body?" you question yourself. "What body? – what form? – what earth – what city? Am I not all of this NOW?" Indeed, in the world of your Mind, that Cosmic One, reality of being has taken place.

Ah, Beloveds, when you return from this journey to the limitations of your mortal self, the realization of a humble master will be yours. In that instant of cosmic consciousness, your awareness and sensitivities are spiritually quickened. You desire to give more – and more – and more – of Him, who so recently was blazingly alive within yourself. Your evaluations will be on a higher plane, as once you have been quickened by the Holy Light, the atoms, elements and molecules within your body are altered in their vibrational frequency. You were united with the Master vibration!

The Mind of your body, which had ruled you through mortal will bows low before the Mind of the King, and the Will of the Lord. Through Cosmic eyes you view the limited world in which you had lived. You discover new manners in which you can become the brother of your brother – and demonstrate greater fellowship with the minds of christs. From that moment forward mortal mind will be supplanted by the superconscious, and your tasks will be pleasurable and filled with joy of service. You witnessed the star in the east, and have "come to worship Him." In all ways, your service to humanity will be as a master, to walk ever more in the holy precepts. You have become one with Him through the minds of Christs. Your words will not be the words of "he who talks and does nothing" – but will be words of Power – the Power of the cosmic-conscious one, awake in the world of man! The radiating energies flowing from you will be cosmic-light energies of highest frequencies. The 'virtue which goes forth' from you, will be in the name and power of Love in its divinest attribute. The eyes of the Soul will look out on the world of man with gentleness and the power of a compassionate Christ!

You shall say, "I am the King – the King of my own world, and as I walk the highway of life with my fellowmen I shall be as a brother to him, – as it was intended in the ever-ever beginning! I have seen Him! I have seen the image within myself, in the radiant light of Being, and in each day of my life, which is left to me to walk, amongst my brothers and sisters, I shall attend to my Father's business. He is reflected in me – and I have seen Him, while yet apart from Him. I now understand my Christ's words, that 'he shall be ever with me, in myself.'"

Dearly Beloveds – are you ready – are you able – are you sincere – in overcoming the first three steps for the glorious and holy fourth? We read the question of your mind. "But – how can I reach this point? What do I DO? What step is there for me to take – in what manner do I approach this altar?"

In this fourth point on the Pathway, Beloved Ones, no generality of method can be given. Illumination is of a personal nature – sacred – holy and transcendental to the Ego whose experience it becomes, and whose Temple is enlivened by its divine fulfillment. There are many requisites for this attainment, – the greatest of which are: LOVE --- DEVOTION – HUMILITY – SACREDNESS OF PURPOSE – and infinite patience and perseverance. The 'method' of attaining this condition, is through the first three steps of the Ladder; – Concentration, meditation and the route of Contemplation.

If you have not procrastinated during the first three phases, and have overcome the obstacles on the path, your bowed head at the fourth phase is the diploma for your admittance to the King.

The material preparations consist of having moved through the first steps as outlined. Having followed the practice of rhythmic breath – up to this point, the stillness of the imperceptible breath will be noted. The psychic and spiritual selves seem to live apart from the conscious breath, and you are placid in your state of wellbeing.

In the fourth Step you do <u>not</u> approach His altar with questions or problems, as you did in the probationary phase. You have come to the place of "no thought" which we spoke of in our first discourse. In this silent and holy state of your consciousness the body identifications are minimized your identity being with God-soul. The momentary thought will be, "this body belongs to someone, but it is not mine, – for it is not the true "I." That Self, which is "I" is the transcendent one, the Christ-of-God." You rejoice with the lightness of the egoic soul. You feel yourself being lifted up – up – up from the heart centre through the top of your head, and moving out from the Rooftop into spheres of no limitations. The breath of your mortal self will seem unrelated to the real 'I' as you become SOUL-CONSCIOUS in the realm of Soul. When the sensation of inner and outer breathing makes itself known, you will wonder at the gentleness of the breath of the 'I' (superconscious), – while the mortal self continues its existence without effort on your part. This condition is the beginning of release from finite self – release from mortal sense limitations, – freedom to explore and ascend into higher spheres of cosmic vibration. The ascendancy is a mortal condition, unobstructed and unfettered.

If you believe --- and persist --- if you are determined ---the humanitarian brotherhood of Christ is in your heart --- you SHALL attain the state of cosmic consciousness through Samadhi. It can be brought about by the conditioning of mortal mind, into the master personality.

Which pathway have you chosen, Beloved Ones? The easy road of procrastination – content with just a "little bit" – a temporary 'flash' or infrequent glimpses of the Third Heaven? Or – is the task too difficult, and the road too steep for your goal in this life time? The choice is yours and the prize is the highest. The Pearl of Great Price is <u>not</u> brought to a disciple without sacrifice. If He is not resurrected in you in this life – then perhaps another? – and another? – or still another?

Love ye one another, as I have loved ye, – the Christ." Ah, now is the time for love, as it is only in the world of form, where you can love – as He loved us all. Brother and sister must walk side by side as brother and sister – IN the world, to know OF the world. To love as HE loved while IN the world – cannot be accomplished until one has known Him, and realized how He loved! He can only be cosmically known, through union with the master soul-mind within yourself. Have ye heard the message – of the Master's Heart?

"Many are called – but few are chosen."

Be thou at Peace, faithful to Him who sent thee. Be thou assured that in each endeavour of thy life, thy call is heard, – for in thyself, thou art alone, in thy call to Him. Be thou mindful of the Star, That One in thee which shall be lifted up to the Greater One, the Soul Star of the Eternal Kingdom, Raise thy soul-eyes and see the light from His star and feel the caress of His love upon thy endeavours.

Christ knoweth every sheep, and each Shepherd who tendeth His flock, knoweth His own. Art thou one of His Sheep – or that one who runneth from the shepherd?

Only thou knowest – thou who readeth the words, and becometh – or becometh not. Abide thou now, in the Light of His countenance, and the warmth of His Love.

So be it!

Master T.

Conclusion

The affirmations included with this Treatise will be beneficial in strengthening your power through suggestion. Use them at your convenience and alter them to suit your own personality. It will assist in transferring the reality of Oneness to your subconscious.

> I AM ONE, IN MIND, BODY AND SOUL – united with my Spiritual Self in all things which I do, He the Christ, lives in me, moves through me, feels – thinks – acts – knows – senses – speaks – hears – and abides in me, as I abide in Him. Although I am dual in all natures and functions, they are ONE in my body. In my actions, thoughts or desires, I shall KNOW that His Mind in me, is greater than mine, and shall hear and KNOW him, for daily He will become more real to me. I give thanks that this is so!
> Amen

This affirmation will assist you before and after your period of Concentration. It would be well to repeat it several times just before retiring: -

> I AM CAPABLE of sending and holding to one thought – at one time. I am able to receive in the same manner. My thoughts shall be channeled with directiveness and move straight on the path. They shall take no side roads or be led into channels unproductive for good. He, the Beloved, shall move through me and flow through me with each thought – as we unite as one – STRONG – ASSURED – JOYOUS AND BELOVED! I give thanks!
> Amen